PIANO • VOCAL • GUITAR

2000-2009 BEST POP SONGS

TEN YEARS OF SHEET MUSIC HITS!

T0055442

Alfred

Produced by
Alfred Music Publishing Co., Inc.
P.O. Box 10003
Van Nuys, CA 91410-0003
alfred.com

Printed in USA.

No part of this book shall be reproduced, arranged, adapted, recorded, publicly performed, stored in a retrieval system, or transmitted by any means without written permission from the publisher. In order to comply with copyright laws, please apply for such written permission and/or license by contacting the publisher at alfred.com/permissions.

ISBN-10: 0-7390-6880-6
ISBN-13: 978-0-7390-6880-9

Alfred Cares. Contents printed on 100% recycled paper.

CONTENTS

Title	Artist	Page
1, 2, 3, 4	Plain White T's	4
21 Guns	Green Day	11
Almost Lover	A Fine Frenzy	18
Be Without You	Mary J. Blige	24
Beautiful World (We're All Here)	Jim Brickman and Adam Crossley	30
Because of You	Kelly Clarkson	36
Boulevard of Broken Dreams	Green Day	42
Chariot	Gavin DeGraw	60
Clumsy	Fergie	48
Complicated	Avril Lavigne	56
Crazy	Gnarls Barkley	65
Crush	David Archuleta	70
Dance with My Father	Luther Vandross	86
Dilemma	Nelly featuring Kelly Rowland	78
Don't Stop the Music	Rihanna	91
Everything	Michael Bublé	98
Falling Slowly	The Swell Season	104
Family Affair	Mary J. Blige	110
The Game of Love	Santana featuring Michelle Branch	117
Gold Digger	Kanye West featuring Jamie Foxx	122
Graduation (Friends Forever)	Vitamin C	127
Haven't Met You Yet	Michael Bublé	134
Hey There Delilah	Plain White T's	158
Hips Don't Lie	Shakira featuring Wyclef Jean	142
Hot N Cold	Katy Perry	152

Title	Artist	Page
I Didn't Know My Own Strength	Whitney Houston	165
I Kissed a Girl	Katy Perry	170
I Turn to You	Christina Aguilera	174
If Everyone Cared	Nickelback	180
Inside Your Heaven	Carrie Underwood	185
Leavin'	Jesse McCartney	190
Live Your Life	T.I. featuring Rihanna	195
My Immortal	Evanescence	204
My Life Would Suck Without You	Kelly Clarkson	209
New Soul	Yael Naïm	216
One Step at a Time	Jordin Sparks	222
Party in the U.S.A.	Miley Cyrus	228
Photograph	Nickelback	234
Smile	Uncle Kracker	240
Soak Up the Sun	Sheryl Crow	246
Stickwitu	Pussycat Dolls	253
The Story	Brandi Carlile	260
This Is It	Michael Jackson	266
Umbrella	Rihanna	270
We Belong Together	Mariah Carey	277
What About Now	Daughtry	284
What Goes Around . . . Comes Around	Justin Timberlake	290
Whatever You Like	T.I.	297
Wild Horses	Susan Boyle	304
You Pulled Me Through	Jennifer Hudson	316
You Raise Me Up	Josh Groban	311

1, 2, 3, 4

Words and Music by
TOM HIGGENSON

1, 2, 3, 4 - 7 - 1

© 2008 WB MUSIC CORP. and SO HAPPY PUBLISHING
All Rights Administered by WB MUSIC CORP.
All Rights Reserved

Verse:
A
___ me more lov - in' that I've ev - er had,___ make___ it all bet - ter when I'm
___ me more lov - in' from the ver - y start,___ piece___ me back to - geth - er when I
Bm
feel - ing sad,___ tell___ me that I'm spe - cial e - ven when I know___ I'm not.___
fall a - part,___ tell___ me things you nev - er e - ven tell your clos - est friends.___
A
A7
D
___ Make___ it feel good___ when it
___ Make___ it feel good___ when it
A
hurts so bad,___ bare - ly get mad.
hurts so bad,___ best___ that I've had.
I'm___ so glad___ I found___

Bm
A
you. I love be - ing a - round you. You make it eas -
G
A
y. It's eas - y as one, two, There's on - ly
one, two, three, four.
Chorus:
D
A/C♯
Bm7
A
one thing two do, three words four you:
(One, two, three, four.
G
Gm6
D
I love you. There's on - ly
I love you.)

1, 2, 3, 4 - 7 - 3

A/C♯
Bm7
A
one way two say those three words, and that's what I'll do.
(One, two, three, four.
G
Gm6
D
1.
I love you. Give
I love you.)
2.
G
Gm6
D
I love you.
A
Bm

A
A7
D
A
Bm
A
G
You make_ it eas - y.
A
D
There's on - ly one thing_
It's eas - y as one, two, *one, two, three, four.* (One,

A/C♯
Bm7
A
G
two do, three words four you:
two, three, four.
Gm6
D
N.C.
D
I love you. There's on - ly one way
I love you.) (One,
A/C♯
Bm7
A
G
two say those three words, and that's what I'll do.
two, three, four.
Gm6
D
A/C♯
Bm7
I love you.
I love you.)

A
G
Gm6
D
I love you.
(I love you.)
A/C♯
Bm7
(One, two, three,
A
G
Gm6
D
four.
I love you.
I love you.)
G
Gm6
D
(I love you.)
I love you.

1, 2, 3, 4 - 7 - 7

21 GUNS

Lyrics by
BILLIE JOE

Music by
GREEN DAY

© 2009 WB MUSIC CORP. and GREEN DAZE MUSIC
All Rights Administered by WB MUSIC CORP.
All Rights Reserved

B♭
C
your - self suf - fo - cat - ing?
breaks the spir - it of your soul.
Verses 2 & 4:
Dm
B♭
F
C
2. Does the pain weigh out the pride?
4. Your faith walks on bro - ken glass,
Dm
B♭
F
C
Dm
B♭
And you look for a place to hide?
and the hang - o - ver does - n't pass.
Did some - one break your
Noth - ing's ev - er
F
C
B♭
C
heart in - side? You're in ru - ins.
built to last, you're in ru - ins.

Chorus:
F
C/E
Dm
C
B♭
F
One, twen - ty - one guns, lay down your arms, give up the fight.
(Ah.
f
C
F
C/E
Dm
C
)
One, twen - ty - one guns, throw up your arms
B♭
F
C
in - to the sky, you and I.
(Ah.
)
B♭
F
1.
C
2.
C
(Ah.
)

Bridge:
Dm
B♭
F
C
Dm
B♭
Did you try to live on your own, when you burned down the
f
F
A
Dm
B♭
F
A
house and home? Did you stand too close to the fi - re? Like a li -
B♭
Csus
C
ar look - ing for for - give - ness from a stone.
Guitar solo:
F
C/E
Dm
C
B♭
F
f

C
F
C/E
Dm
C
B♭
F
C
B♭
F
A
Dm
B♭
F
C
Dm
B♭
F
C
subito mp
Verse 5:
Dm
B♭
F
C
Dm
B♭
5. When it's time to live and let die, and you can't get an -
mf

16
F
C
Dm
B♭
oth - er try.
Some - thing in - side this
F
C
B♭
heart has died, you're in ru - ins.
Chorus:
F
C/E
Dm
C
B♭
F
One, twen - ty - one guns, lay down your arms, give up the fight.
(Ah.
f
C
F
C/E
Dm
C
One, twen - ty - one guns, throw up your arms
)

B♭ F C F C/E
in - to the sky.
(Ah.)
One, twen - ty - one guns,
Dm C B♭ F C
lay down your arms,
give up the fight.
(Ah.)
F C/E Dm C B♭ F
One, twen - ty - one guns,
throw up your arms
in - to the sky,
(Ah.
C B♭ F C
you and I.
(Ah.)

ALMOST LOVER

Words and Music by
ALISON SUDOL

© 2007 WB MUSIC CORP. and AMPSTAR MUSIC
All Rights Administered by WB MUSIC CORP.
All Rights Reserved

Pre-chorus:
Am
F/A
G
trick.
Well, I'd nev - er want to see you un -
mp
C
Dm
G
hap-py. I thought you'd want the same
for me.
for me.
Chorus:
C
G
Good - bye, my al - most lov - er.
Good - bye, my hope - less dream.
mf
Dm
F
I'm try - ing not to think a - bout you.
Can't you just let me be?

C
G
So long, my luck - less ro - mance. My back is turned on you.
Dm
F
To Coda
Should have known you'd bring me heart - ache. Al - most lov - ers al - ways
C
Verse 2:
Am
do.
2. We walked a - long a crowd - ed street. You took my
dim.
mp
F
Am
hand and danced with me; im - ag - es.

F
Am
And when you left, you kissed my lips. You told me you would
F
Am
nev - er, nev - er for - get these im - ag - es, oh no.
dim.
D.S. 𝄋 al Coda
F
Well, I'd
𝄌 Coda
C
Bdim
do.
Bridge:
Am
G
I can - not go to the o - cean. I can - not drive the streets at
mf

F
Em
night. I can - not wake up in the morn - ing with - out you on my mind.
Am
G
So you're gone and I'm haunt - ed, and I'll bet you are just
F
Dm
fine. Did I make it that eas - y to walk right in and out of my
mp
a tempo
G
Chorus:
C
life?
Good - bye, my al - most lov - er.
mp

G
C
Dm
Good-bye, my hope-less dream.
I'm try-ing not to think a-bout you.
F
C
Why can't you just let me be?
So long, my luck-less ro-mance.
cresc.
mf
G
Dm
My back is turned on you.
Should have known you'd bring me heart-ache.
F
C
Al-most lov-ers al-ways do.
mp

BE WITHOUT YOU

Words and Music by
BRYAN MICHAEL COX, JOHNTA AUSTIN,
MARY J. BLIGE, and JASON PERRY

© 2005 W.B.M. MUSIC CORP., NOONTIME SOUTH, INC., BABYBOY'S LITTLE PUBLISHING COMPANY, CHRYSALIS MUSIC,
NAKED UNDER MY CLOTHES MUSIC, UNIVERSAL MUSIC CORP., MARY J. BLIGE MUSIC and JASON'S LYRICS
All Rights on Behalf of itself, NOONTIME SOUTH, INC. and BABYBOY'S LITTLE PUBLISHING COMPANY Administered by W.B.M. MUSIC CORP.
All Rights Reserved

C
Am
Dm
Gm7
We did - n't deal noth - in' o - ver - night 'cause a love like this takes some time.
C
Am7
Dm7
B♭
Peo - ple swore it off as a phase, said we can't see that, now
C
Am7
Dm7
Gm7
from top to bot-tom, they see that we did that. (Yes) It's so true that (yes) we've been through it,
Chorus:
C
A7
Dm
B♭maj7
(yes) we got real sh**. See, ba - by, we've been too strong for too long, and I can't be with - out

C
Am7
Dm
Gm7
you, ba - by. And I'll be wait-ing up un - til you get home, 'cause I can't sleep with - out
C
A7
Dm
B♭maj7
you, ba - by. An - y - bod - y who's ev - er loved, ya know just what I feel.
C
Am7
Dm
Gm7
To Coda
Too hard to fake it, noth-ing can re-place it. Call the ra - di - o if you just can't be with - out
1.
C
A7
your ba - by.
2.
C
A7
your ba - by.

Bridge:
Gm7
Am7
B♭maj7
Am7
See, this is real talk, c - 'mon, al - ways stay, (no mat - ter what,) good or
Gm7
Am7
B♭maj7
A7
bad, (thick or thin,) right or wrong (all day, ev - 'ry day.) Now if you're
N.C.
down on love or don't be - lieve, this ain't for you. And if you got it
(No, this ain't for you.
deep in your heart, and deep down you know that it's true, well, let me see you put your
C - 'mon, c - 'mon, c - 'mon.

28
Dm
B♭maj7
C
Am7
hands up,
Hands up, fel - las, tell your la - dy she's the one.
fel - las, tell your la - dy she's the one.
Oh, put your
Dm
Gm7
C
A7
D.S.𝄋 al Coda
hands up,
Hands up, la - dies, let him know he's got you locked.)
look him right in the eyes and tell him we've been
𝄌 Coda
C
A7
Dm
B♭maj7
your ba - by.
C
Am7
Dm
Gm7
C
A7

Verse 2:
I've got a question for you,
(See, I already know the answer.)
Still, I wanna ask you:
Would you lie? *(no)*
Make me cry? *(no)*
Do somethin' behind my back and then try to cover it up?
Well, neither would I, baby.
My love is only your love, *(yes)*
I'll always be faithful. *(yes)*
I'm for real *(yes)*
And with us you'll always know the deal.
(To Chorus:)

BEAUTIFUL WORLD

(We're All Here)

Words and Music by
ADAM CROSSLEY

© 2009 UNIVERSAL TUNES, a division of UNIVERSAL INC./BRICKMAN SONGS (SESAC),
DOGBOY MUSIC (ASCAP) and BEAUTIFUL PRINCESS PUBLISHING (ASCAP)
Print Rights for BRICKMAN SONGS Administered Worldwide by ALFRED MUSIC PUBLISHING CO., INC.
All Rights Reserved

A
C♯m/G♯
F♯m7
C♯m/G♯
A
D6/9
E
ev - 'ry - one.
You fell a - sleep un - der the
D6/9
E
A
C♯m/G♯
cher - ry tree.
La la la la la la,
F♯m7
A/E
Dmaj9
A/E
A
C♯m/G♯
F♯m7
C♯m/G♯
it's a beau - ti - ful world and we're all here.
Verse 2:
A
C♯m/G♯
F♯m7
C♯m/G♯
A
C♯m/G♯
2. Your win - ter skin, warm-ing in the sum - mer sun.
mf

F♯m7
C♯m/G♯
A
C♯m/G♯
F♯m7
C♯m/G♯
(Sum - mer sun.) We know, with - in, you will stay for -
A
C♯m/G♯
F♯m7
C♯m/G♯
A
D6/9
ev - er young. (For - ev - er young.) You fell a - sleep
E
D6/9
E
un - der the star - lit sea. It's time to wake up.
Chorus:
A
A(9)/C♯
D6/9
A/E
E
A
A(9)/C♯
The moon is high a - bove you. We're all here 'cause

D6/9
A/C♯
E/B
F♯m
A/E
Dmaj9
A/C♯
we love you. And when you fi - nal - ly o - pen your eyes
Bm9
Dmaj9
Esus
E
A
C♯m/G♯
and ears, you'll see and you'll hear us sing. La la la la la la,
To Coda
F♯m7
A/E
Dmaj9
A/E
E
A
C♯m/G♯
it's a beau - ti - ful world and we're all here. La la la la la la,
F♯m7
A/E
Dmaj9
A/E
E
F♯m7
E/G♯
it's a beau - ti - ful world and we're all here. La la la la la la,

Dmaj9
Esus
A
C♯m/G♯
It's a beau - ti - ful world.
F♯m7
C♯m/G♯
A
C♯m/G♯
A7/G
F♯m7
It's a beau - ti - ful world.
Bridge:
Dm/F
A/E
D6
Esus
Ba ba ba ba.
(Ooh,
Ah.
Ba ba ba ba ba.
ooh.
D6
E
D6
E
D.S. 𝄋 al Coda
You fell a - sleep un - der the sol - id sea. It's time to wake up.

Coda
A
E/B
A(9)/C♯
D6/9
Esus
F♯m7(4)
La la la la la la, it's a beau - ti - ful world and we're all here.
A
C♯m/G♯
F♯m7
A/E
Dmaj9
A/E
E
La la la la la la, it's a beau - ti - ful world and we're all here.
F♯m7
E/G♯
Dmaj9
Esus
A
C♯m/G♯
La la la la la la,
it's a beau-ti - ful world.
mp
F♯m7
C♯m/G♯
A
C♯m/G♯
F♯m7
C♯m/G♯
A
(It's a beau-ti - ful world.)
It's a beau-ti - ful world.

BECAUSE OF YOU

Words and Music by
KELLY CLARKSON, BEN MOODY
and DAVID HODGES

© 2004 FSMGI (IMRO), SMELLSLIKEMETAL PUBLISHING (BMI), SMELLY SONGS (ASCAP), and 12:06 PUBLISHING (BMI)
All Rights for FSMGI (IMRO) and SMELLSLIKEMETAL PUBLISHING (BMI) Administered by STATE ONE MUSIC AMERICA (BMI)
All Rights for SMELLY SONGS (ASCAP) Controlled and Administered by EMI APRIL MUSIC, INC.
All Rights For 12:06 PUBLISHING (BMI) Controlled and Administered by EMI BLACKWOOD MUSIC, INC.
All Rights Reserved

Fm(9)
Fm
E♭
A♭
Cm
cause my heart so much mis - er - y.
I will not break the way
cause I know that's weak - ness in your eyes.
I'm forced to fake a smile,
you did, you fell so hard.
I've learned the hard way to
a laugh ev - 'ry day of my life.
My heart can't pos - si - bly break when it
E♭sus
nev - er let it get that far.
was - n't e - ven whole to start with.
Be - cause of
cresc.
Chorus:
D♭
you, I nev - er stray too far from the side - walk.
Be - cause of
mf

Fm
D♭
E♭
C7
you, I learned to play on the safe side, so I don't get hurt. Be - cause of
B♭m7
A♭/C
E♭
C7
you, I find it hard to trust not on - ly me, but ev-'ry - one a - round me. Be - cause of you,
D♭maj9
1.
E♭(9)
I am a - fraid.
2.
E♭
Bridge:
Cm
Fm
I watched you die, I heard you cry ev - 'ry night in your
(I watched you

E♭sus
E♭
Cm
Fm
sleep. I was so young, you should have known bet - ter than to lean
die in your sleep. I was too
A♭/E♭
Cm
Fm
on me. You nev - er thought of an - y - one else, you just saw
young for you to lean on me. You nev - er
E♭sus
E♭
A♭/E♭
Cm
Fm
your pain. And now I cry in the mid-dle of the night for the
saw me.)
E♭sus
E♭
E♭sus
E♭
Fm/E♭
E♭
same damn thing. Be - cause of

Chorus:
Fm
D♭
E♭sus
you, I nev - er stray too far from the side - walk. Be - cause of
mp
Fm
D♭
E♭sus
N.C.
you, I learned to play on the safe side so I don't get hurt. Be - cause of
cresc.
Gm
E♭
F
Fsus
F
you, I try my hard - est just to for - get ev - 'ry - thing. Be - cause of
mf
Gm
E♭
F
D7
you, I don't know how to let an - y - one else in. Be - cause of you,

Cm7
B♭/D
F
D7
I'm a-shamed of my life be-cause it's emp - ty. Be-cause of you
E♭maj9
F
I am a - fraid. Be - cause of you.
Gm
E♭
F
Ah, be - cause of you.
mp
Gm
E♭
F
Ooh, ooh.

BOULEVARD OF BROKEN DREAMS

Words by
BILLIE JOE

Music by
GREEN DAY

© 2004 WB MUSIC CORP. and GREEN DAZE MUSIC
All Rights Administered by WB MUSIC CORP.
All Rights Reserved

Fm
A♭
E♭
B♭
Don't know where it goes, but it's home to me and I walk a - lone.
mind. On the bor - der - line of the edge and where I walk a - lone.
I walk this emp - ty street on the bou - le - vard of bro - ken dreams,
Read be - tween the lines of what's f***ed up and ev - ery - thing's al -
where the cit - y sleeps and I'm the on - ly one and I walk a - lone.
right. Check my vi - tal signs and know I'm still a - live and I walk a - lone.

Fm
A♭
E♭
B♭
Fm
A♭
I walk a - lone, I walk a - lone.
Chorus:
E♭
B♭
A♭/C
D♭
A♭
I walk a - lone, I walk a...
My shad - ow's the on -
E♭
Fm
D♭
A♭
ly one that walks be - side me.
My shal - low heart's
E♭
Fm
D♭
A♭
the on - ly thing that's beat - ing.
Some - times I wish

E♭ Fm D♭ A♭
To Coda
some - one out there will find me. 'Til then I walk
C N.C. Fm A♭ E♭ B♭
a - lone. Ah. Ah. Ah. Ah.
Fm A♭ 1. E♭ B♭ 2. E♭ B♭ A♭/C
Ah. Ah. Ah. I walk a - lone, I walk a...
D♭ A♭ E♭ Fm D♭ A♭
(Gtr. solo...

E♭
Fm
D♭
A♭
E♭
Fm
D♭
A♭
C
N.C.
...end solo)
Verse 3:
Fm
A♭
E♭
B♭
3. I walk this emp - ty street on the bou - le - vard of bro - ken dreams,

D.S. 𝄋 al Coda
Fm
A♭
E♭
B♭
A♭/C
where the cit - y sleeps and I'm the on - ly one and I walk a...
Coda
C
a - lone.
F5
D♭
E♭2
B♭/D
f
1.2.3.
A♭5
E5
4.
A♭5
E5

CLUMSY

Words and Music by
BOBBY TROUP, WILL ADAMS
and STACY FERGUSON

© 2007 EMI ROBBINS CATALOG INC., WILL I AM MUSIC, INC., CHERRY RIVER MUSIC CO., HEADPHONE JUNKIE PUBLISHING and EMI APRIL MUSIC, INC.
All Rights on behalf of itself and WILL I AM MUSIC, INC. Administered by CHERRY RIVER MUSIC CO.
All Rights on behalf of itself and HEADPHONE JUNKIE PUBLISHING Administered by EMI APRIL MUSIC, INC.
{This Song Contains a Sample of ***"THE GIRL CAN'T HELP IT,"*** by BOBBY TROUP, © 1956 (Renewed) EMI ROBBINS CATALOG INC.}
Exclusive Print Rights for EMI ROBBINS CATALOG INC. Administered by ALFRED MUSIC PUBLISHING CO., INC.
All Rights Reserved

N.C.
by. Oh, ba - by.
Can't help it, the girl can't help it. Can't help it.
(Drums)
Verse:
C
Dm7/C
C
Dm7/C
1. First time that I saw your eyes, boy, you
2. Can't breathe when you touch my sleeve; but - ter -
C
Dm7/C
C
Dm7/C
looked right through me, mmm, mmm.
flies so cra - zy, mmm, mmm.
C
Dm7/C
C
Dm7/C
Play it cool, but I knew you knew that
Whoa now, think I'm go - in' down; friends don't

C
Dm7/C
C
N.C.
cu - pid hit me, mmm, mmm.
know what's with me, mmm, mmm.
(Bkgrd.) You got me
Chorus:
C
Dm7/C
C
Dm7/C
trip - pin', Oh. stum - bl - in', Oh. flip - pin', Oh. fum - bl - in'. No.
C
Dm7/C
C
Dm7/C
Clum - sy 'cause I'm fall - in' in love.
In, in, love, love. You got me
C
Dm7/C
C
Dm7/C
slip - pin', Oh. tum - bl - in', Oh. flip - pin', sink - in', Oh. fum - bl - in'. No.

C
Dm7/C
C
N.C.
Clum - sy 'cause I'm fall - in' in love.
In, in, love, love.
So in
So in
C
love with you.
love with you.
(Bkgrd.) Can't help it, the girl can't help it.
Oh, ba - by.
Oh, no.
Can't help it, the girl can't help it.
Oh, no.
Oh, please.
1.
N.C.
2.
N.C.
Oh, how.
Oh, no.
Can't help it, the girl can't help it.
Can't help it.
Can't help it.
(Drums)
(Drums)
Bridge:
C
Am
F/A
(Spoken:) You know, this ain't the first time this has happened to me, this lovesick thing.
I like serious relationships and a, huh, a
(Bkgrd.) Ooh, hoo, hoo, hoo.
Ooh, hoo, hoo, hoo.
Ooh, hoo, hoo, hoo.

G/B
C
Am
girl like me don't stay single for long.
Ooh, hoo, hoo, hoo.
'Cause every time a boyfriend and I break up, my world is crushed and I'm all alone.
Ooh, hoo, hoo, hoo.
Ooh, hoo, hoo, hoo.
F/A
G/B
C
The love bug crawls right back up and bites me, and I'm back.
Ooh, hoo, hoo, hoo.
Ooh, hoo.
(Bkgrd.) Can't help it, the girl can't help it.
In love.
Can't help it, the girl can't help it.
Oh, God.
Can't help it, the girl can't help it.
I'm back in love.
N.C.
C
Can't help it.
Whoo.
Can't help it, the girl can't help it.
I'm back in love
(Drums)

___ now. I'm back in love___ now, ba - by. I'm back in love_
Can't help it, the girl can't help it. Can't help it, the girl can't help it.
Chorus:
N.C.
C
Dm7/C
___ now. And now you got me. Oh.___ Oh.___
Can't help it. You got me trip - pin', stum - bl - in',
C
Dm7/C
C
Dm7/C
flip - pin', Oh.___ fum - bl - in'. No.___ Clum - sy 'cause I'm fall - in' in
C
Dm7/C
C
Dm7/C
love.___ Oh.___ Oh.___
In, in, love, love. You got me slip - pin', tum - bl - in',

C
Dm7/C
C
Dm7/C
sink - in', Oh. fum - bl - in'. No. Clum - sy 'cause I'm fall - in' in
C
N.C.
C
Dm7/C
C
Dm7/C
love. So in love with you.
In, in, love, love.
C
Dm7/C
C
Dm7/C
Clum - sy 'cause I'm fall - in' in love.
In, in, love, love. You got me
C
Dm7/C
C
Dm7/C
slip - pin', Oh. tum - bl - in', Oh. sink - in', Oh. fum - bl - in'. No.

C
Dm7/C
C
N.C.
Clum - sy 'cause I'm fall - in' in love.
So in
In, in, love, love.
C
Dm7/C
C
Dm7/C
love with you.
So in
C
Dm7/C
C
N.C.
love with you.
So in love with you.
(Drums)

COMPLICATED

Gtr. tuned down 1 whole step:
⑥ = D ③ = F
⑤ = G ② = A
④ = C ① = D

Words and Music by
LAUREN CHRISTY, GRAHAM EDWARDS,
SCOTT SPOCK and AVRIL LAVIGNE

Moderately slow rock ♩ = 80

© 2002 WARNER-TAMERLANE PUBLISHING CORP., PRIMARY WAVE TUNES,
WB MUSIC CORP., PRIMARY WAVE SONGS, ALMO MUSIC CORP. and AVRIL LAVIGNE PUBLISHING LTD.
All Rights on behalf of itself and PRIMARY WAVE TUNES Administered by WARNER-TAMERLANE PUBLISHING CORP.
All Rights on behalf of itself and PRIMARY WAVE SONGS Administered by WB MUSIC CORP.
All Rights Reserved

C(9)
B♭(9)
Dsus
Csus
D
C
And if you could on - ly let it be, you will see
Where you are ain't where it's at. You see, you're mak - ing me
...end solo)

G
F
Em7
Dm7
I like you the way you are when we're driv - ing in your car
laugh out when you strike your pose. Take off all your prep - py clothes.
Chill out, what - cha yell - ing for? Lay back, it's all been done be - fore.

C(9)
B♭(9)
Dsus
Csus
D
C
and you're talk - ing to me one on one. But you be - come
You know you're not fool - ing an - y - one when you be - come
And if you could on - ly let it be, you will see

C(9)
B♭(9)
Em
Dm
some - bod - y else 'round ev - 'ry - one else. You're watch - ing your back like you can't re - lax. You're
C(9)
B♭(9)
D5
C5
try'n' to be cool, you look like a fool to me. Tell me
Chorus:
Em7
Dm7
C(9)
B♭(9)
G
F
Dsus
Csus
D
C
why'd you have to go and make things so com - pli - cat - ed? See, the way you're
Em7
Dm7
C(9)
B♭(9)
G
F
Dsus
Csus
D
C
act - ing like you're some-bod - y else gets me frus - trat - ed. Life's like this, you,

Em7
Dm7
C(9)
B♭(9)
G
F
Dsus
Csus
D
C
you fall and you crawl and you break and you take what you get and you turn it in - to
Am9
Gm9
1.
C2
B♭2
hon - es - ty. Prom-ise me I'm nev - er gon - na find ya fake it. No, no,
G5
F5
2.
C2
B♭2
no. it. No, no,
3.
C2
B♭2
D.S. 𝄋
4.
C2
B♭2
it. No, no. it. No, no, no.

CHARIOT

Words and Music by
GAVIN DeGRAW

© 2003 WARNER-TAMERLANE PUBLISHING CORP. and G. DEGRAW MUSIC, INC.
All Rights Administered by WARNER-TAMERLANE PUBLISHING CORP.
All Rights Reserved

Em7
C(9)
G
D
is choc-'late - cov - ered cher-ries
and seed-less wa - ter - mel - on.
Oh,
Em7
C(9)
G
A7
noth-ing from the ground is good e - nough.
Bod - y, rise,
Chorus:
Am7(♭5)
G
Bm7
look what's o - ver me.
Oh, char - i - ot,
Em7
C(9)
G
Bm7
Em7
C(9)
your gold - en waves are walk - ing down up - on this face.

G
B7
Em7
C(9)
G
Bm7
To Coda
Oh, char - i - ot, I'm sing - ing out loud to guide me.
1.
Em7
C(9)
Em7
C(9)
G
D
Give me your strength.
Em7
C(9)
G
D
2.
Em7
C(9)
Give me your strength.
G
Bridge:
F
C
You'll be my va - ca - tion a - way from this place.

G
D
F
You know what I want.
Hold-ing that cup
D.S. 𝄋 al Coda
C
D
C(9)
D
C(9)/E
D/F♯
that's pour-ing o-ver the sides.
You make me want to spread my arms and fly.
Coda
Em7
C(9)
G
Bm7
Em7
C(9)
Give me your strength. Give me your strength.
Char-i-ot,
G
Bm7
Em7
C(9)
G
Bm7
give me your strength.
Char-i-ot,
give me your strength.
(Lead vocal ad lib.)

Verse 2:
Remember seeking moon's rebirth?
Rains made mirrors of the earth.
The sun was just yellow energy.
There is a living promise land,
Even over fields of sand.
Seasons fill my mind and cover me.
Bring it back.
More than a memory.
(To Chorus:)

CRAZY

Words and Music by
THOMAS DECARLO CALLAWAY, BRIAN JOSEPH BURTON,
GIANFRANCO REVERBERI and GIAN PIERO REVERBERI

© 2006 WARNER/CHAPPELL MUSIC PUBLISHING LTD., CHRYSALIS MUSIC LTD. and BMG RICORDI MUSIC PUBLISHING SpA
All Rights for WARNER/CHAPPELL MUSIC PUBLISHING LTD. in the U.S. and Canada Administered by WARNER-TAMERLANE PUBLISHING CORP.
"Crazy" contains samples from ***"Last Man Standing"*** by GIANFRANCO REVERBERI and GIAN PIERO REVERBERI
All Rights Reserved

A♭
Gsus
ech - o in so much space.
Mm,
G
Cm
mm, mm.
And when you're out there with - out
2.3. See additional lyrics
E♭maj7
care, yeah, I was out of touch.
And it
A♭(9)
was - n't be - cause I did - n't know e - nough.

A♭
Gsus
G
I just knew too much, mm. Does that make me cra -
Chorus:
Cm
E♭maj7
zy? Does that makes me cra - zy?
A♭maj7
Does that make me cra - zy? Pos - si - bly.
Gsus
To Coda
G
C
And I hope that you are hav-

A♭(9)
A♭
ing the time of your life.
But think twice.
E♭maj7
Gsus
That's my on - ly ad - vice.
1.
G
2.
G
D.S. 𝄋 al Coda
Mm.
𝄌 Coda
G
C
Mm,
ooh,

Verse 2:
Come on now, who do you, who do you,
Who do you, who do you think you are?
Ha ha ha, bless your soul,
You really think you're in control.

Chorus 2:
Well, I think you're crazy.
I think you're crazy.
I think you're crazy,
Just like me.
My heroes had the heart to lose their lives out on a limb,
And all I remember is thinking I want to be like them.

Verse 3:
Ever since I was little, ever since I was little it looked like fun.
And it's no coincidence I've come,
And I can die when I'm done.

Chorus 3:
But maybe I'm crazy.
Maybe you're crazy.
Maybe we're crazy.
Probably.
(To Coda)

CRUSH

Words and Music by
EMANUEL KIRIAKOU,
DAVID HODGES and JESS CATES

© 2008 RODITIS MUSIC, INC., 12:06 PUBLISHING and RIGHT BANK MUSIC, INC.
All Rights for RODITIS MUSIC, INC. Administered by ARTHOUSE ENTERTAINMENT, LLC
All Rights for 12:06 PUBLISHING Controlled and Administered by EMI BLACKWOOD MUSIC, INC.
All Rights Reserved Used by Permission

Bm7 Cm7
F♯m Gm
G2 A♭2
D5 E♭5
A/C♯ B♭/D
It was a rush. What a rush. 'Cause the
pos - si - bil - i - ty that you would ev - er feel the same way a - bout me,
it's just too much, just too much. Why do I keep
run - ning from the truth? All I ev - er think a - bout is you. You got me hyp-

Bm7
Cm7
F♯m
Gm
G2
A♭2
D5
E♭5
no-tized, so___ mes - mer-ized, and I just got to know.___ Do you
cresc.
Chorus:
G2
A♭2
D
E♭
Bm7
Cm7
Asus
B♭sus
ev - er think, when you're all a-lone, all that we could be, where this thing could go?_____ Am I
mf
G2
A♭2
D
E♭
Bm7
Cm7
Asus
B♭sus
cra - zy or___ fall - ing___ in love? Is it real or just___ an - oth - er crush?___ Do you
G2
A♭2
D
E♭
Bm7
Cm7
Asus
B♭sus
catch a breath when I look at you? Are you hold-ing back like the way I do?_____ 'Cause I'm

G2
A♭2
D
E♭
Bm7
Cm7
A
B♭
try - in', try'n' to walk a - way, but I know this crush ain't go - ing a - way,
e - yeah, e - yeah, e - yeah, e - yeah. Go - ing a - way,
e - yeah, e - yeah, e - yeah, e - yeah. 2. Has it
Verse 2:
F♯m
Gm
D5
E♭5
A/C♯
B♭/D
ev - er crossed your mind, when we're hang - ing, spend - ing time, girl, are we just friends?
mp

Bm7
Cm7
F#m
Gm
G2
A♭2
3
D5
E♭5
A/C#
B♭/D
Is there more?
Is there more?
See, it's a
chance we've got - ta take, 'cause I be - lieve that we can make this in - to
some - thing that - 'll last, last for - ev - er, for - ev - er. Do you
cresc.
Chorus:
G2
A♭2
D
E♭
Bm7
Cm7
Asus
B♭sus
ev - er think, when you're all a - lone, all that we could be, where this thing could go? Am I
mf

G2
A♭2
D
E♭
Bm7
Cm7
Asus
B♭sus
cra - zy or fall - ing in love? Is it real or just an - oth - er crush? Do you
G2
A♭2
D
E♭
Bm7
Cm7
Asus
B♭sus
catch a breath when I look at you? Are you hold-ing back like the way I do? 'Cause I'm
To Coda
G2
A♭2
D
E♭
Bm7
Cm7
A
B♭
try - in', try'n' to walk a - way, but I know this crush ain't go - ing a - way,
G2
A♭2
D
E♭
Bm7
Cm7
A
B♭
e - yeah, e - yeah, e - yeah, e - yeah. Go - ing a - way,

G2
A♭2
D
E♭
Bm7
Cm7
A
B♭
e - yeah, e - yeah, e - yeah, e - yeah.
Why do I keep

Bridge:
G2
A♭2
Bm7
Cm7
A
B♭
run - ning from the truth? All I ev - er think a - bout is you. You got me hyp-

G2
A♭2
D.S. 𝄋 al Coda
no - tized, so mes - mer-ized, and I just got to know. Do you

Coda
G2
A♭2
D
E♭
Bm7
Cm7
A
B♭
e-yeah, e-yeah, e-yeah e-yeah.
Go-ing a-way,
G2
A♭2
D
E♭
Bm7
Cm7
A
B♭
e-yeah, e-yeah, e-yeah, e-yeah.
Go-ing a-way,
Repeat ad lib. and fade
G2
A♭2
D
E♭
Bm7
Cm7
A
B♭
e-yeah, e-yeah, e-yeah, e-yeah.
Go-ing a-way,

DILEMMA

Words and Music by
KENNY GAMBLE, BUNNY SIGLER,
CORNELL HAYES and ANTOINE MACON

© 2002 WARNER-TAMERLANE PUBLISHING CORP., JACKIE FROST MUSIC, BMG SONGS, INC. and SUGA SHACK MUSIC
{This song contains elements of ***"LOVE, NEED AND WANT YOU,"*** by KENNY GAMBLE and BUNNY SIGER, © 1982 WARNER-TAMERLANE PUBLISHING CORP.}
All Rights Reserved

Gm7
C
Am7
Dm
when I'm with my boo, boy, you know I'm cra - zy o - ver you. No
Gm7
C
Am7
Dm
mat - ter what I do, all I think a - bout is you. E - ven
Gm7
C
Am7
Dm
when I'm with my boo, you know I'm cra - zy o - ver you.
Verse:
Gm7
C
(Nelly:)
1. I met this chick and she just moved right up the block from me, and
2. See additional lyrics

Am7
Dm
Gm7
C
she got the hots for me, the fin - est thing my hood did see. But oh, no, oh, no, she got a man and a
Am7
Dm
Gm7
C
son, though, oh. But that's o - kay, 'cause I wait for my cue and just lis - ten, play my po - si - tion, like a
Am7
Dm
Gm7
C
short - stop, pick up - e'r' - 'thing ma - mi hit - tin', and in no time, I bet I make this one
Am7
Dm
Gm7
C
mine. And that's for sure, 'cause I, I nev - er been the type to break up a hap - py home, but

Am7
Dm
Gm7
C
there's some-thin' 'bout ba - by girl___ I just can't leave a - lone.
So tell me, ma, what's it gon - na be?___ She said,
Chorus:
Am7
Dm
Gm7
C
No mat - ter what___ I do,___ all I
(Kelly:) "You don't know what you mean to me."_____
Am7
Dm
Gm7
C
think a - bout___ is you.___ E - ven when I'm with___ my boo,___ boy, you know I'm
Am7
Dm
Gm7
C
cra - zy o - ver you.___ No mat - ter what___ I do,_____ all I

Am7
Dm
Gm7
C
1.
Am7
Dm
think a - bout is you. E - ven when I'm with my boo, you know I'm cra - zy o - ver you.
2.
Bridge:
Am7
Dm
Gm7
C
Am7
Dm
cra - zy o - ver you. And I love you, and I need you. Nel-ly, I
Gm7
C
Am7
Dm
love you, I do, and it's more than you'll
Gm7
C
Am7
Dm
ev - er know, boy, it's fo' sho. You can

Gm7
C
Am7
Dm
al - ways count on my love for - ev - er more, yeah,
(Nelly:)
yeah. East coast, I know you shak-in' right. Down South, I know you bounc-in' right.
West coast, I know you walk-in' right. Mid - west, I see you swing-in' right.
(Kelly:) You don't know what you mean to me. No
Chorus:
(Kelly:)
mat - ter what I do, all I think a - bout is you. E - ven

Gm7
C
Am7
Dm
when I'm with my boo, boy, you know I'm cra - zy o - ver you. No
mat - ter what I do, all I think a - bout is you. E - ven
when I'm with my boo, you know I'm cra - zy o - ver you.
(Nelly:) East coast, I know you shak-in' right. Down South, I know you bounc-in' right.

Verse 2:
I see a lot and you look and I never say a word.
I know how niggaz start actin' trippin' out here about they girls.
And there's no way Nelly gon' fight over no dame, as you could see.
But I like your steez, your style, your whole demeanor.
The way you come through and holla and swoop me in his two-seater.
Now that's gangstah and I got special ways to thank ya.
Don't you forget it but, it ain't that easy for you to pack up and leave him.
But you and dirty got ties for different reasons.
I respect that and right before I turn to leave, she said,
"You don't know what you mean to me."
(To Chorus:)

DANCE WITH MY FATHER

Words and Music by
RICHARD MARX and LUTHER VANDROSS

© 2002 CHI-BOY MUSIC, UNCLE RONNIE'S MUSIC, INC. and EMI APRIL MUSIC, INC.
All Rights on behalf of itself and UNCLE RONNIE'S MUSIC, INC. Administered by EMI APRIL MUSIC, INC.
All Rights for CHI-BOY MUSIC outside the U.S. and Canada Administered by WB MUSIC CORP.
All Rights Reserved

E♭
E♭/F
F
and dance with my moth - er and me, and then
Then fi - nal - ly, make me do just what my ma - ma said.
B♭/D
E♭
E♭m/G♭
spin me a - round till I fell a - sleep, then up the stairs he would car -
Lat - er that night, when I was a - sleep, he left a dol - lar un - der
B♭/F
C/E
Fsus
F
ry me. And I knew for sure I was loved. If
my sheet. Nev - er dreamed that he would be gone from me. If
Chorus:
B♭
F/A
Gm
I could get an - oth - er chance, an - oth - er walk, an -
I could steal one fi - nal glance, one fi - nal step, one

E♭
Cm
Gm
oth - er dance_ with him,
fi - nal dance_ with him,
I'd play a song that would nev - er, ev - er end.
How
'Cause
I'd love,
E♭
Fsus
F
1.
B♭
love, love
to dance with my fa - ther a - gain.
F/A
Gm
E♭
2.
B♭
2. When
Bridge:
E♭
F
B♭
F/A
Some-times, I'd lis - ten out - side her door,
and I'd hear how my moth - er cried

Gm
E♭
Fsus
F
for him.
I pray for her e - ven more than me.
Cm7
Fsus
F
I pray for her e - ven more than me.
B♭
F/A
Gm
E♭(9)
I
Chorus:
C
G/B
Am
know I'm pray - in' for much too much, but could you send back the

F
Dm
Am
on - ly man she loved? I know you don't do it u - su - al - ly, but, dear Lord,
F
Gsus
G
Am
she's dy - in' to dance with my fa - ther a - gain.
Dm11
Fm6
Ev - 'ry night I fall a - sleep, and this is all I ev - er dream.
C
G/B
F
Dm7
G7sus
G
C
rit.

DON'T STOP THE MUSIC

Words and Music by
MICHAEL JACKSON, MIKKEL STORLEER ERIKSEN,
TOR ERIK HERMANSEN and FRANKIE STORM

© 2007 MIJAC MUSIC, INC., SONY/ATV MUSIC PUBLISHING LTD. and DABNEY MUSIC PUBLISHING
All Rights for MIJAC MUSIC Administered by WARNER-TAMERLANE PUBLISHING CORP.
{This song contains samples of ***"WANNA BE STARTIN' SOMETHIN',"*** by MICHAEL JACKSON, © 1982 MIJAC MUSIC, Administered by WARNER-TAMERLANE PUBLISHING CORP.}
All Rights Reserved

F♯m
fa-v'rite place. I got-ta get my bod-y mov-in', *shake* the stress a-way. I was-n't
look-in' for no-bod-y when you looked my way. Pos-si-ble can-di-date, yeah.
Verses 2 & 3:
D
2. Who knew that you'd be up in here, look-in' like you do? You're
mu-sic.
3. Ba-by, are you read-y? 'Cause it's get-ting close.
sim.
F♯m
mak-in' stay-in' o-ver here im-pos-si-ble. Ba-by, I must say your au-ra is in-
Don't you feel the pas-sion read-y to ex-plode. What goes on be-tween us, no one

D
cred - i - ble. If you don't have to go, don't.
has to know. This is a pri - vate show, oh.
Do you know what you start - ed?
I just came here to par - ty, but now we're rock - in' on the dance floor, act - in' naugh-ty.
F♯m
Your hand's a - round my waist. Just let the mu - sic play. We're hand in hand, chest to
𝄋 Chorus:
D
chest, and now we're face to face. I wan - na take you a - way. Let's es - cape in - to the

F♯m
mu - sic.___ D J, let___ it play. I just can't re - fuse it. Like the way you
do this. Keep on rock - in' to it. Please don't stop the, please don't stop the mu - sic.
D
I wan - na take you___ a - way. Let's es-cape in - to the mu - sic.___ D J, let___ it
F♯m
play. I just can't re - fuse it. Like the way you do this. Keep on rock - in'

1.
to it. Please don't stop the, please don't stop the, please don't stop the
2.3.
D
please don't stop the, please don't stop the mu - sic.
Ma ma se ma ma sa ma ma coo sa, ma ma
se ma ma sa ma ma coo sa. Ma ma se ma ma sa ma ma coo sa, ma ma
F♯m
Please don't stop the mu - sic.
se ma ma sa ma ma coo sa. Ma ma se ma ma sa ma ma coo sa, ma ma

To Coda
se ma ma sa ma ma coo sa. Ma ma se ma ma sa ma ma coo sa, ma ma
N.C.
Please don't stop the mu - sic.
se ma ma sa ma ma coo sa. Ma ma se ma ma sa ma ma coo sa, ma ma
se ma ma sa ma ma coo sa. Ma ma se ma ma sa ma ma coo sa, ma ma
Please don't stop the mu - sic.
se ma ma sa ma ma coo sa. Ma ma se ma ma sa ma ma coo sa, ma ma

D.S. 𝄋 al Coda

Coda

EVERYTHING

Words and Music by
MICHAEL BUBLÉ, ALAN CHANG
and AMY FOSTER

© 2006 I'M THE LAST MAN STANDING MUSIC, IHAN ZHAN MUSIC, SONGS OF UNIVERSAL, INC. and ALMOST OCTOBER SONGS
All Rights for I'M THE LAST MAN STANDING MUSIC Administered by WB MUSIC CORP.
All Rights for IHAN ZHAN MUSIC Administered by WARNER-TAMERLANE PUBLISHING CORP.
All Rights Reserved

D Bm7 E7 G G/A
ming pool on an Au - gust day, and you're the per - fect thing to say.
ter - y, you're from out - er space, you're ev - 'ry min - ute of my ev - 'ry
D A7sus D Bm7 E7
And you play it coy, but it's kind of cute, ah, when you
day. And I can't be - lieve, ah, that I'm you're man, and I
Gm A7sus D A7sus D Bm7
smile at me, you know ex - act - ly what you do. Ba - by, don't pre - tend that you don't know
get to kiss you, ba - by, just be - cause I can. What - ev - er comes our way, ah, we'll see
E7 Gm A7sus D
it's true. 'Cause you can see it when I look at you.
it through, and you know that's what our love can do.
And in this cra -

Chorus:
G A D Bm7 G A
zy life, and through these cra - zy times,
D D7 G F#7(b9) Bm D/A
it's you, it's you. You make me sing. You're ev - 'ry line,
E7 Gm Em7(b5)/A 1. D Bm7
you're ev - 'ry word, you're ev - 'ry - thing.
E7 Gm Em7(b5)/A D A7sus
2. You're a car -

2.
D
Bm7
E7
Gm
Em7(♭5)/A
D
(Inst. solo ad lib....
Bm7
E7
Gm
Em7(♭5)/A
D
...end solo)
So
Bm7
E7
Gm
Em7(♭5)/A
D
la la la la la la la.
So
Bm7
E7
Gm
A7(♭9)
D N.C.
la la la la la la la.
And in this

Chorus:
Amaj7
B
E
C♯m7
A
B
cra - zy life, and through these cra - zy times,
E
E7
A
G♯7
C♯m
E/B
it's you, it's you. You make me sing. You're ev - 'ry line,
F♯7
Am6
C♯m
C♯m7/B
you're ev-'ry word, you're ev-'ry - thing.
F♯7
You're ev - 'ry song, and I sing a-long,

Am6
F♯m7(♭5)/B
E
C♯m7
'cause you're my ev - 'ry - thing.
F♯7
A
A/B
E
C♯m7
F♯7
A
A/B
E
C♯m7
So la la
F♯7
Am
F♯m7(♭5)/B
E
la la la la la. So
Freely
C♯m7
F♯7
Am
E
la la la la la la la la la la la.

FALLING SLOWLY

(from *Once*)

Words and Music by
GLEN HANSARD and
MARKETA IRGLOVA

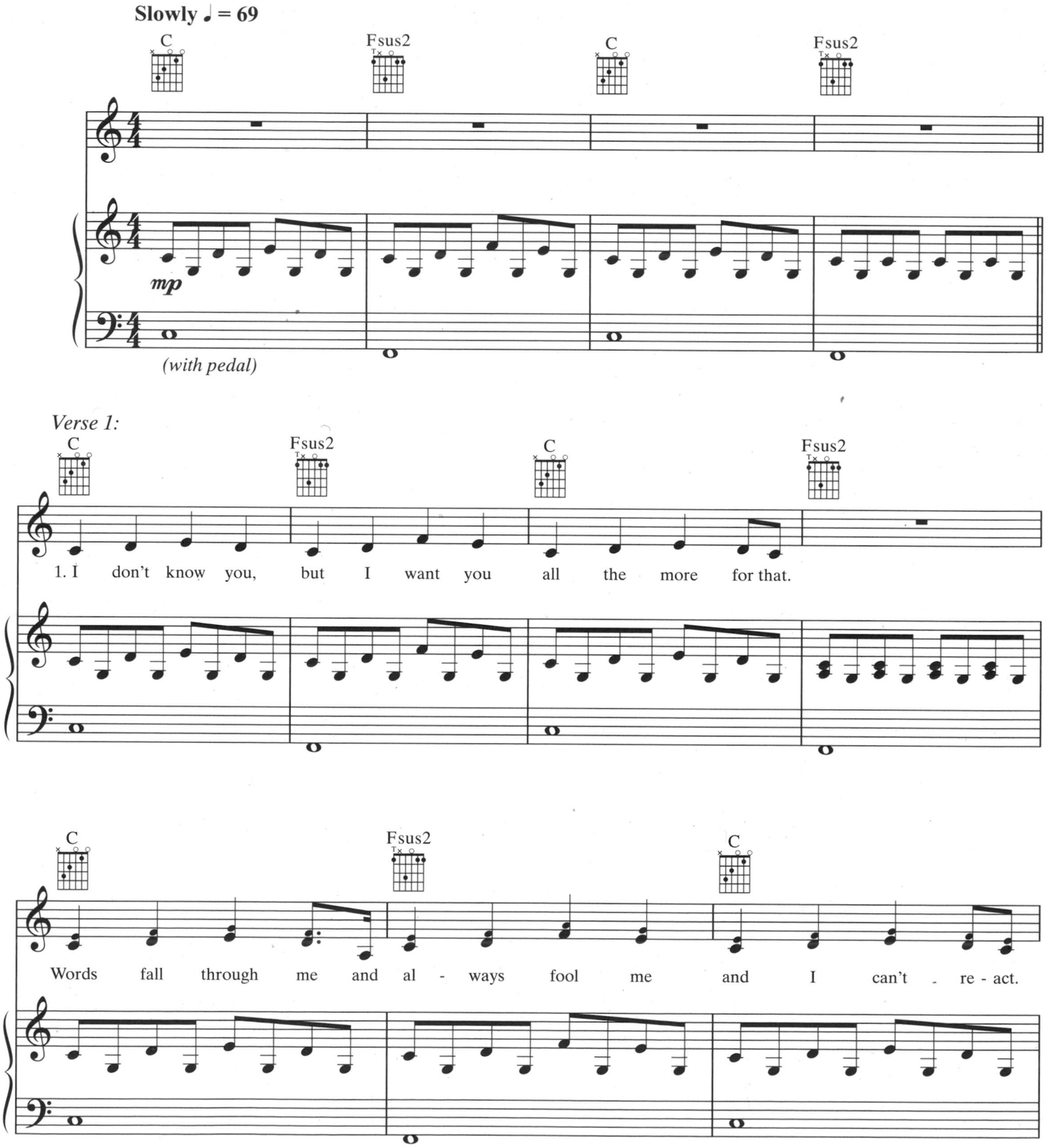

© 2006 THE SWELL SEASON PUB DESIGNEE
All Rights Administered by WB MUSIC CORP.
All Rights Reserved

Fsus2
Am7
G
Fsus2
G
Games that nev - er a - mount to more than they're
Am7
G
F(9)
Fsus2
meant will play them-selves out.
cresc.
Chorus:
C
Fsus2
Am7
Take this sink - in' boat and point it home, we've still got
mf
Fsus2
C
Fsus2
time.
Raise your hope - ful voice, you have a

Am7
Fsus2
choice, you make it now.
decresc.
Verse 2:
C
Fsus2
C
2. Fall - ing slow - ly, eyes that know me and I can't go back.
mp
Fsus2
C
Fsus2
C
Moods that take me and e - rase me and I'm paint - ed black.
Fsus2
Am
Em/G
Fsus2
G
Well, you have suf-fered e - nough and warred with your -

Am
Em/G
F(9)
Fsus2
self. It's time that you won.
cresc.
Chorus:
C
Fsus2
Am7
Take this sink - in' boat and point it home, we've still got
mf
Fsus2
C
Fsus2
time.
Raise your hope - ful voice, you have a
Am7
Fsus2
C
choice, you've made it now.
Fall - in' slow - ly,

Fsus2
Am7
Fsus2
sing your mel - o - dy, I'll sing it loud.
C
Fsus2
Am7
(Strings)
Fsus2
G/F
8va
Take it all.
Fsus2
I paid the cost too late,
now you're gone.

G/F
F(9)
(Strings)
Fsus2
C
mp
Fsus2
C
Fsus2
C
rit.

FAMILY AFFAIR

Words and Music by
ANDRE YOUNG, MELVIN BRADFORD,
MARY J. BLIGE, MICHAEL ELIZONDO,
CAMARA KAMBON, LUCHANA LODGE,
ASIAH LOUIS and BRUCE MILLER

© 2001 WB MUSIC CORP., HARD WORKING BLACK FOLKS INC., MELVIN BRADFORD MUSIC, AIN'T NOTHING BUT FUNKIN' MUSIC,
UNIVERSAL MCA MUSIC PUBLISHING, MARY J. BLIGE MUSIC, MUSIC OF WINDSWEPT, BLOTTER MUSIC, ELVIS MAMBO MUSIC,
COLORSCAPES PUBLISHING, LUCHI PUBLISHING CO., ASIAHTOWN ENT. and SPIRIT ONE MUSIC
All Rights on behalf of itself, HARD WORKING BLACK FOLKS INC., MELVIN BRADFORD MUSIC
and AIN'T NOTHING BUT FUNKIN' MUSIC Administered by WB MUSIC CORP.
All Rights Reserved

C♯m
me. Don't need no hat - er - a - tion, holl - a - ra - tion in this danc - er -
G♯m7
y. Let's get it per - cu - lat - in' while ' ya wait - in' so just dance for
Verses 1 & 2:
C♯m
me. 1. Come on, ev - 'ry - bod - y, get on up, 'cause ya know we gots ta get it crunk.
2. See additional lyrics
G♯m7
Mar - y J. is in the spot to - night and I'm - a make you feel al - right.

C♯m
Come on, ba - by, just par - ty wit me, let loose and set your bod - y free.
G♯m7
Leave your sit - u - a - tions at the door, so when you step in - side, jump on the floor.
Chorus:
C♯m
Let's get it crunk up - on, have fun up - on, up in this danc - er -
G♯m7
y. We got y'all o - pen now, ya float - in' so ya gots to dance for

C♯m
me. Don't need no hat - er - a - tion, holl - a - ra - tion in this danc - er -
G♯m7
y. Let's get it per - cu - lat - in' while ya wait - in' so just dance for
Verse 3:
C♯m
3. We____ don't need____ no hat - ers. We're just
me.
G♯m7
try - ing to love____ one an - oth - er. We just

C♯m
want y'all to have a good time, no more dra - ma in your life. Work real
G♯m7
hard to make a dime. If ya got beef, your prob-lem, not mine. Leave all
C♯m
that B. S. out - side. We gon - na cel - e - brate all night. Let's have
G♯m7
fun to - night, no fights. Turn that Dre track way up high. Mak - in' ya

C♯m
dance all night and I got some real heat for ya this time. It does - n't
G♯m7
mat - ter if you're white or black. Let's get crunk, 'cause Mar - y's back.
Chorus:
C♯m
Let's get it crunk up - on, have fun up - on, up in this danc - er -
G♯m7
y. We got y'all o - pen now, ya float - in' so ya gots to dance for

Verse 2:
It's only going to be about a matter of time
Before ya get loose and start to lose your mind.
Cop you a drink, go ahead and rock ya ice,
'Cause we're celebrating no more drama in our life.
With the Dre track pumpin', everybody's jumpin'.
Go ahead and twist ya back and get body bumpin'.
I told ya, leave your situations at the door.
So grab somebody and get your ass on the dance floor.
(To Chorus:)

THE GAME OF LOVE

(featuring Michelle Branch)

Words and Music by
GREGG ALEXANDER and RICK NOWELS

© 2002 KEEPIN' IT REAL HOW 'BOUT YOU MUSIC and FUTURE FURNITURE MUSIC
All Rights for FUTURE FURNITURE MUSIC Administered by SPIRIT MUSIC GROUP
All Rights for KEEPIN' IT REAL HOW 'BOUT YOU MUSIC Administered by FINTAGE PUBLISHING AND COLLECTION B.V.
All Rights Reserved

Dmaj9
Em9
Dmaj9
So, please tell me (1.3.) why don't you come a - round
So, please, ba - by, (2.) try and use me for what
Gmaj7
Em7/A
Em9
no more. 'Cause right now I'm 1. cry - 3. dy -
I'm good for. It ain't say - ing good - bye,
F♯m7
Gmaj7
Em7/A
ing ing out - side the door of your 1. can - dy 3. lov - ing store.
it's knock - ing down the door of your can - dy store.
It just takes a
Chorus:
Em9
Dmaj9
Em9
lit - tle bit of this, a lit - tle bit of that. It start - ed with a kiss, now we're

Dmaj9
Em9
Dmaj9
up to bat. A lit - tle bit of laughs, a lit - tle bit of pain. I'm
To Coda
1.
2.
Em9
Em7/A
Em7/A
tell - ing you, my babe, it's all in the game of love. in the game of love.
Em9
Dmaj9
Gmaj7
It's all in this game of love.
Bridge:
Em7/A
Bm7
F♯m7
You roll me, con - trol me, con -

120
Gmaj7
Em7/A
Em9
sole me. Please hold me. You guide me, di -
F♯m7
Gmaj7
Em7/A
vide me in two, whoa.
Em9
Dmaj9
Em9
(Guitar solo...
Dmaj9
Em9
Dmaj9
1.
2.
D.S. 𝄋 al Coda
Gmaj7
Em7/A
Em7/A
3. So, please tell me
...end solo)

Coda
Em7/A
Em9
Dmaj9
in the game of love.
It's all in this game of love.
Em9
Dmaj9
Em9
It's all in the game of love.
Dmaj9
Gmaj7
Em7/A
Let's play the game of love.
Repeat ad lib. and fade

GOLD DIGGER

Words and Music by
RAY CHARLES, RENALD RICHARD
and KANYE WEST

© 2005 UNICHAPPELL MUSIC INC., MIJAC MUSIC, EMI BLACKWOOD MUSIC INC. and PLEASE GIMME MY PUBLISHING INC.
{This song contains samples of *"I GOT A WOMAN,"* by RAY CHARLES and RENALD RICHARD, © 1954 (Renewed) MIJAC MUSIC, UNICHAPPELL MUSIC, INC.}
All Rights on behalf of itself and MIJAC MUSIC Administered by UNICHAPPELL MUSIC INC.
All Rights Reserved

She gives me mon - ey when I'm in need.
but she ain't mess-in' with no broke n**-**z.
Now, I ain't say-in' she's a gold dig-ger,
D♭7
I got - ta leave, I got - ta
but she ain't mess-in' with no broke n**-**z.
Get down, girl, go 'head, get down.
To Coda
leave, I got - ta leave, I got - ta
Get down, girl, go 'head, get down.
Get down, girl, go 'head, get down.
Verse:
A♭7
4
leave. Yeah, she gives me mon - ey when I'm in need.
Get down, girl, go 'head.
1. Cutie, the bomb, met her at a beauty salon with a
2.3. See additional lyrics

She gives me mon - ey when I'm in need.
baby Louis Vuitton under her underarm. She said, "I can tell you rock, I can tell by your charm. Far as
D♭7
I got - ta leave, I got - ta
girls, you got a flock, I can tell by your charm and your arm." But I'm lookin' for the one Have you seen her? My
leave, I got - ta leave, I got - ta
psychic told me she had have an ass like Serena, Trina, Jennifer Lopez. Four kids, and I
A♭7
4
leave. Yeah, she gives me mon - ey when I'm in need.
gotta take all they bad ass to show biz. Ok, get your kids, but then they got their friends. I

She gives me mon - ey when I'm in need.
pulled up in the Benz, they all got up in. We all went to Den and then I had to pay. If you
D♭7
I got - ta leave, I got - ta
f***in' with this girl, then you better be paid. You know why? It take too much to touch her.
leave, I got - ta leave, I got - ta
From what I heard, she got a baby by Busta. My best friend say she used to f*** with Usher.
1.2.
D.S. 𝄋
3.
D.S. 𝄋 al Coda
leave. Yeah, she gives me mon - leave. Yeah, she gives me mon -
I don't care what none of ya'll say, I still love her.

Verse 2:
Eighteen years, eighteen years,
She got one of your kids, got you for eighteen years.
I know somebody payin' child support for one of his kids.
His baby momma's car and crib is bigger than his.
You will see him on TV any given Sunday.
Win the Super Bowl and drive off in a Hyundai.
She was s'pposed to buy your shorty Tyco with your money.
She went to the doctor, got lypo with your money.
She walkin' around, lookin' like Michael with your money.
Should of got that insured, Geico for your money.
If you ain't no punk, holler, "We want prenup."
We want prenup, yeah.
It's something that you need to have,
'Cause when she leave your ass she gone leave with half.
Eighteen years, eighteen years,
And on her 18th birthday, he found out it wasn't his.
(To Chorus:)

Verse 3:
Now, I ain't sayin' you a gold digger, you got needs.
You don't want your dude to smoke, but he can't buy weed.
You go out to eat and he can't pay, ya'll can't leave.
There's dishes in the back, he gotta roll up his sleeves.
But why ya'll washin', watch him.
He gone make it into a Benz out of that Datsun.
He got that ambition, baby, look in his eyes.
This week he moppin' floors, next week it's the fries.
So, stick by his side.
I know his dude's ballin' but, yeah, that's nice.
And they gone keep callin' and tryin',
But you stay right, girl.
But when you get on, he leave your ass for a white girl.
(To Chorus:)

GRADUATION

(Friends Forever)

Words and Music by
COLLEEN FITZPATRICK
and JOSH DEUTSCH

© 1999 WARNER-TAMERLANE PUBLISHING CORP., BIG BLACK JACKET MUSIC and BLANC E MUSIC
All Rights on behalf of itself and BIG BLACK JACKET MUSIC Administered by WARNER-TAMERLANE PUBLISHING CORP.
All Rights Reserved

C G Am E
leave this year, we won't be com-ing back. No more hang-ing out 'cause we're on a dif-f'rent track and if you
F C F G
got some-thing that you need to say, you'd bet-ter say it right now 'cause you don't have an-oth-er day. 'Cause we're
C G Am E
mov-ing on and we can't slow down. These mem-o-ries are play-ing like a film with-out sound and I
2.3. See additional lyrics
F C F G
keep think-ing of that night in June. I did-n't know much of love but it came too soon. And there was

C G Am E
me and you and when we got real blue, we'd stay at home, talk-ing on the tel - e-phone, and we would
F C F Gsus G
To Coda
get so ex - cit - ed and we'd get so scared, laugh-ing at our-selves, think-ing life's not fair.
Chorus:
C G Am E
And this is how it feels...
As we go on, we re - mem - ber
F C F G C G
all the times we had to - geth - er.
And as our lives change,

1.
Am E F C F G C G
come what - ev - er, we will still be friends for - ev - er.
Am E F C F C/G G
2. So if we
2.
F G C G/B
friends for - ev - er. La la la la la la la la.
Am E F C F G
La la la la la la la la. La la la la la la la la. Yeah, yeah,

C
G/B
Am
E
La la la la la la la la.
La la la la la la la la.
yeah.
F
C
F
G
G7
La la la la la la la.
(We will still be friends for - ev - er.)
Cm
Cm/B♭
A♭maj7
Cm/G
Fm
Cm/E♭
Fm/A♭
G
Cm
Cm/B♭
A♭maj7
Cm/G
Fm
Cm/E♭

A♭
Gsus
G
C
D.S. 𝄋 al Coda
3. Will we
Coda
F
G
C
G
keep on think - ing it's our time to fly.
As we go on,
Am
E
F
C
F
G
we re - mem - ber all the times we had to - geth - er.
C
G
Am
E
F
C
And as our lives change, come what - ev - er, we will still be

Verse 2:
So if we get the big jobs and we make the big money,
When we look back at now, will our jokes still be funny?
Will we still remember everything we learned in school,
Still be trying to break every single rule?
Will little brainy Bobby be the stockbroker man?
Can Heather find a job that won't interfere with her tan?
I keep, keep thinking that it's not goodbye,
Keep on thinking it's our time to fly.
And this is how it feels…
(To Chorus:)

Verse 3:
Will we think about tomorrow like we think about now?
Can we survive it out there, can we make it somehow?
I guess I thought that this would never end,
And suddenly it's like we're women and men.
Will the past be a shadow that will follow us around?
Will the memories fade when I leave this town?
I keep, keep thinking that it's not goodbye,
Keep thinking it's our time to fly.
(To Chorus:)

HAVEN'T MET YOU YET

Words and Music by
MICHAEL BUBLÉ, ALAN CHANG
and AMY FOSTER

© 2009 WB MUSIC CORP., I'M THE LAST MAN STANDING MUSIC, INC., WARNER-TAMERLANE PUBLISHING CORP., IHAN ZHAN MUSIC and MS. DOE MUSIC
All Rights on behalf of itself and I'M THE LAST MAN STANDING MUSIC, INC. Administered by WB MUSIC CORP.
All Rights on behalf of itself, IHAN ZHAN MUSIC and MS. DOE MUSIC Administered by WARNER-TAMERLANE PUBLISHING CORP.
All Rights Reserved

G♭maj7
E♭m9
B♭m7
A♭
prised, not ev - 'ry-thing lasts. I've bro-ken my heart so man-y times, I've stopped
wait. I'll nev - er give up. I guess it's half tim - ing and the oth - er half's
D♭
G♭maj7
E♭m9
keep-ing track. Talk my - self in, I talk my-self out, I get all worked up,
luck. Wher - ev-er you are, when-ev - er it's right, you'll come out of no -
A♭
B♭/D
E♭m7
D♭/F
then I let my - self down. I tried so ver - y hard not to lose it.
where and in - to my life. And I know that we can be so a - maz - ing.
E♭m7
A♭
E♭m7
I came up with a mil - li - on ex - cus - es. I thought I thought of
And, ba - by, your love is gon - na change me. And now I can see

D♭/F
G♭
A♭
ev - 'ry pos - si - bil - i - ty.
ev - 'ry pos - si - bil - i - ty.
And I know some - day
And some - how, I know
Chorus:
G♭maj7
A♭
D♭
G♭maj7
A♭
that it - 'll all turn out.
You'll make me work so we can work to work it out.
B♭m
E♭m7
F7
B♭m7
D♭7
And I prom - ise you, kid, that I'll give so much more than I get.
G♭
1.
A♭
D♭
G♭maj7
I just have - n't met you yet.
Mm.

E♭m9
B♭m7
A♭
2.
A♭
just have - n't met you
Bridge:
B♭m
F/A
D♭7/A♭
yet. They say all's fair in
E♭7/G
E♭m7
D♭/F
love and war. But I won't need to fight it. We'll
G♭
A♭
get it right and we'll be u - nit - ed.

138
A♭maj7
B♭
E♭
A♭maj7
B♭
Cm
f
A♭maj7
G7
Cm7
E♭7
A♭
B♭
Fm7
E♭/G
Fm7
And I know that we can be so a - maz - ing.
And be - ing in your
mf
B♭
Fm7
E♭/G
life is gon - na change me.
And now I can see ev - 'ry sin - gle pos -

A♭
B♭
si - bil - i - ty, mm.
And some-day I know
Chorus:
A♭maj7
B♭
E♭
A♭maj7
B♭
it - 'll all turn out.
And I'll work to work
mp
Cm
Fm7
G7
Cm7
E♭7
it out.
Prom - ise you, kid,
I'll give more than
A♭
B♭
I get, than I get, than I get, than I get.
Oh, you know
cresc. poco a poco

140
A♭maj7
B♭
E♭
A♭maj7
B♭
it - 'll all turn out. And you'll make me work so we can work to work it out.
f
Cm
Fm7
G7
Cm7
E♭7
And I prom - ise you, kid, to give so much more than I get.
A♭
B♭
E♭
Yeah, I just have - n't met you yet.
mf
A♭maj7
Fm9
Cm7
B♭
I just have - n't met you

E♭
A♭maj7
Fm9
yet. Oh, I prom-ise you, kid, to give so much more than I get.
Cm7
B♭
E♭
A♭maj7
(I said, love, love, love, love,
Fm9
Cm7
B♭
E♭
love, love, love, love, love, love,
I just have-n't met you yet.
A♭maj7
Fm9
Cm7
B♭
E♭
love, love, love, love.) I just have-n't met you yet.

HIPS DON'T LIE

© 2006 SONY/ATV TUNES LLC, HUSS-ZWINGLI PUBLISHING INC., LANFRANCO MUSIC,
JNR MUSIC PUBLISHING, EMI BLACKWOOD MUSIC, INC., TE-BASS MUSIC and CARAMEL HOUSE MUSIC
All Rights for CARAMEL HOUSE MUSIC Administered by ENSIGN MUSIC CORPORATION
All Rights Reserved

G♭
A♭
B♭m
¿Có-mo se lla - ma? (¡Sí!) Bo - ni - ta, (¡Sí!) mi ca - sa, su ca - sa.
Sha - ki - ra, Sha - ki - ra.
G♭
A♭
Fm
Oh, ba - by, when you talk like that, you make a wom - an go___ mad.
G♭
A♭
B♭m
So, be___ wise and keep_ on read - ing the signs of my bod - y.
Chorus:
G♭
A♭
Fm
And I'm on to - night. You know my hips don't lie, and I'm start-ing to feel___ it's right.
and I'm start-ing to feel___ you, boy.

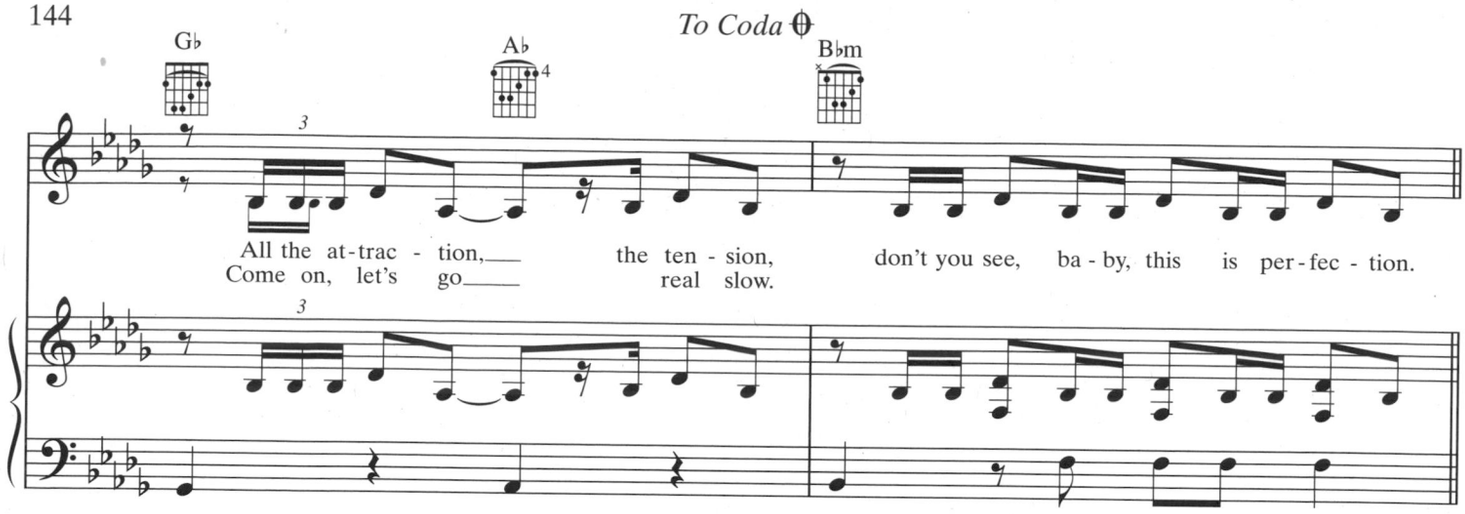
To Coda
G♭
A♭
B♭m
All the at-trac - tion, the ten - sion, don't you see, ba - by, this is per - fec - tion.
Come on, let's go real slow.

Verse 1:

1. Hey, girl, I can see your bod - y mov - ing and it's driv - ing me cra - zy.

And I didn't have the slight - est i - de - a un - til I saw you danc - ing.

And when you walk up on the dance floor, no - bod - y can - not ig - nore the way you move your bod - y, girl.

D.S. al Coda
And ev - 'ry - thing so un - ex - pec - ted, the way you right and left it. So you can keep on shak - ing it.
Coda
B♭m
Don't you see, ba - by, a - sí es per - fec - to?
Chorus:
G♭
A♭
Fm
Oh, I know I'm on to - night, my hips don't lie and I'm start - ing to feel it's right.
G♭
A♭
B♭m
All the at - trac - tion, the ten - sion, don't you see, ba - by, this is per - fec - tion.
Sha - ki - ra, Sha - ki - ra.

Verse 2:

2. Oh, boy, I can see your bod - y mov - ing; half an - i - mal, half man.
I don't, don't real - ly know what I'm do - ing but you seem to have a plan.
My will and self - re - straint have come to fail now, fail now.
See, I'm do - ing what I can, but I can't so you know. That's a bit too hard to ex - plain.

Vocal Break:
B♭m
Bai - la en la ca - lle de no - che. Bai - la en la ca - lle de dí -
a. Bai - la en la ca - lle de no - che. Bai - la en la ca - lle de dí -
I
Pre-chorus:
G♭
A♭
4
Fm
nev - er real - ly knew that she could dance like this. She makes a man_ want to speak Span - ish.
a.
G♭
A♭
4
B♭m
3
3
¿Có-mo se lla - ma? (¡Sí!) Bo - ni - ta, (¡Sí!) mi ca - sa, su ca - sa.
Sha - ki - ra, Sha - ki - ra.

G♭
A♭
Fm
Oh, ba - by, when you talk like that, you know you got me hyp - no - tized.
G♭
A♭
B♭m
So be wise and keep on read - ing the signs of my bod - y.
Bridge:
Se - ño - ri - ta, feel the con - ga, let me see you move like you come from Co - lom - bia.

Mi - ra en Ba - rran-qui - lla se bai - la a - sí, say it! Mi - ra en Ba - rran-qui - lla se bai-la a - sí.

Rap:

Yeah, she's so sexy, every man's fantasy, a refugee like me back with the Fugees from a third world country.

I go back like when 'pac carried crates for Humpty Humpty. I need a whole club dizzy.

Why the C.I.A. wanna watch us? Colombians and Haitians, I ain't guilty, it's a musical transaction.
Ho-bope, se-bope, no more do we snatch ropes. Refugees run the seas 'cause we own our own boats.
Chorus:
B♭m
G♭
A♭
Fm
I'm on to - night, my hips don't lie and I'm start - ing to feel you, boy.
G♭
A♭
B♭m
Come on, let's go real slow. Ba - by, like this is per - fec - to.

G♭
A♭
Fm
Oh, you know, I'm on to - night, my hips don't lie and I'm start-ing to feel it's right.
G♭
A♭
B♭m
The at - trac - tion, the ten - sion, ba - by, like this is per - fec - tion.
E♭m
A♭
Fm
No
fight - ing.
No
G♭
A♭
B♭m
fight - ing.
(let echo)

HOT N' COLD

Words and Music by
KATY PERRY, LUKASZ GOTTWALD
and MAX MARTIN

© 2008 WHEN I'M RICH YOU'LL BE MY BITCH, KASZ MONEY PUBLISHING and UNIVERSAL MUSIC-MGB SONGS
All Rights for WHEN I'M RICH YOU'LL BE MY BITCH Administered by WB MUSIC CORP.
All Rights Reserved

Am
C
al - ways speak cryp - ti - c'lly. I should know
Now, you're plain bor - ing. I should know
G
D
Am
C
that you're no good for me.
that you're not gon - na change.
'Cause you're hot,
Chorus:
G
D
Am
C
then you're cold. You're yes, then you're no. You're in, then you're out. You're up,
mf
G
D
then you're down. You're wrong when it's right. It's black and it's white. We fight,

Am
C
G
D
we break up. We kiss, we make up. (You. You don't real - ly wan - na
Am
C
stay, no. (You. But you don't real - ly wan - na go - o. You're hot,
G
D
Am
C
then you're cold. You're yes, then you're no. You're in, then you're out. You're up,
1.
N.C.
then you're down.
mp

2.
then you're down.
E5
C
G5
D
Bridge:
E5
C
G5
D
Some - one call the doc - tor, got a case of love
E5
C
bi - po - lar. Stuck on a roll - er coast - er and I

G5
D
N.C.
can't get off this ride.
You change your mind
mp
like a girl chang-es clothes.
'Cause you're hot,
Chorus:
G
D
Am
C
then you're cold. You're yes, then you're no. You're in, then you're out. You're up,
mf
G
D
then you're down. You're wrong when it's right. It's black and it's white. We fight,

Am
C
1.
2.
we break up. We kiss, we make up. You're hot, we make up.
G
D
Am
C
(You.) You don't real - ly wan - na stay, no. (You.) But you don't real - ly wan - na
G
D
go - o. You're hot, then you're cold. You're yes, then you're no. You're in,
Am
C
G
then you're out. You're up, then you're down.

HEY THERE DELILAH

Words and Music by
TOM HIGGENSON

© 2005 WB MUSIC CORP., FEARMORE MUSIC and SO HAPPY PUBLISHING
All Rights Administered by WB MUSIC CORP.
All Rights Reserved

G
A
Bm
Times Square can't shine as bright as you. I swear it's
We'll have the life we knew we would. My word is
A
A5
D5
true. Hey there, De - li - lah, don't you
good. Hey there, De - li - lah, I've got
F♯m
D5
wor - ry a - bout the dis - tance, I'm right there. If you get lone - ly, give this
so much left to say. If ev - 'ry sim - ple song I wrote to you would
F♯m
Bm
Bm/A
song an - oth - er lis - ten. Close your eyes.
take your breath a - way, I'd write it all.

G
A
Bm
A
A5
Lis-ten to my voice, it's my dis - guise.
I'm by your side.
E-ven more in love with me, you'd fall.
We'd have it all.
Chorus:
D5
D5/A
Bm
Bm/C♯
D5
D5/A
Oh, it's what you do to me,
oh, it's what you do to me.
mf
Bm
Bm/C♯
D5
D5/A
Bm
Bm/C♯
Oh, it's what you do to me,
To Coda
1.
2.
D5
D5/A
Bm
Bm/C♯
D5
D5/A
Bm
Bm/A
oh, it's what you do to me.
What you do to me.
A

Bridge:
G
A
thou - sand miles seems pret - ty far, but they've got planes and trains and cars. I'd walk
D5
D5/A
Bm
Bm/A
to you if I had no oth - er way. Our
G
A
friends would all make fun of us, and we'll just laugh a - long be - cause we know
D5
D5/C♯
Bm
Bm/A
that none of them have felt this way. De -

G
A
li - lah, I can prom-ise you that by the time we get through, the world
Bm
will nev - er, ev - er be the same, and you're to blame.
A
Verse 3:
D5
F♯m
3. Hey there, De - li - lah, you be good and don't you miss me. Two more

D5
F♯m
Bm
Bm/A
years and you'll be done with school and I'll be mak-ing his - t'ry, like I do.
G
A
Bm
Bm/A
You know it's all be - cause of you.
G
A
Bm
Bm/A
G
A
We can do what - ev - er we want to.
Hey there, De - li - lah, here's to you.
Bm
A
A5
D.S. 𝄋 al Coda
This one's for you.

Coda
Bm
Bm/C♯
D5
D5/A
Bm
Bm/C♯
What you do to me.
Oh,
whoa,
D5
D5/A
Bm
Bm/C♯
D5
D5/A
Bm
Bm/C♯
whoa.
Oh,
whoa, whoa.
Oh,
D5
D5/A
Bm
Bm/C♯
D5
D5/A
D5
oh,
oh.

I DIDN'T KNOW MY OWN STRENGTH

Words and Music by
DIANE WARREN

© 2009 REALSONGS (ASCAP)
All Rights Reserved

D♯m7
C♯(9)
I thought I would break.
I thought I would break.
I did - n't know my own
I did - n't know my own
Chorus:
B(9)
F♯(9)/A♯
G♯m7(4)
F♯sus
F♯
strength, and I crashed down and I tum - bled, but I did not crum - ble.
D♯m7
C♯(9)
I got through all the pain.
I did - n't know my own
B(9)
F♯(9)/A♯
strength, sur - vived my dark - est hour, my faith kept me a - live.

G♯m7(4)
F♯sus
F♯
I picked my - self back up.
I hold my head up high.
D♯m7
C♯(9)
1.
I was not built to break.
I did - n't know my own
B(9)
2.
strength.
I did - n't know my own
Bridge:
G♯m
A♯
strength. There were so man - y times I won-dered how I'd get through the night. I

B
C♯
thought I took all that I could take. I did - n't know my own
Chorus:
B(9)
F♯(9)/A♯
G♯m7(4)
F♯sus
F♯
strength, and I crashed down and I tum - bled, but I did not crum - ble.
mp
mf
D♯m7
C♯(9)
N.C.
I got through all the pain. I did - n't know my own
B(9)
F♯(9)/A♯
strength, my faith kept me a - live.

G♯m7(4)
F♯sus
F♯
I picked my - self back up.
I hold my head up high.
D♯m7
C♯(9)
I was not built to break.
I did - n't know my own
B(9)
Freely
strength.
mp
I was - n't built to break.
D♯m7
C♯
D♯m7
C♯
F♯(9)
I got to know my own strength.

I KISSED A GIRL

Words and Music by
KATY PERRY, LUKASZ GOTTWALD,
MAX MARTIN and CATHY DENNIS

© 2008 WHEN I'M RICH YOU'LL BE MY BITCH, KASZ MONEY PUBLISHING, UNIVERSAL MUSIC-MGB SONGS and EMI MUSIC PUBLISHING LTD.
All Rights for WHEN I'M RICH YOU'LL BE MY BITCH Administered by WB MUSIC CORP.
All Rights Reserved

A5
Bdim
C
Dm7
F5
C/E
It's not what I'm used to, just wan - na try you on.
It's not what good girls do, not how they should be - have.
A5
Bdim
C
Dm7
F5
C/E
I'm cu - ri - ous, for you caught my at - ten - tion.
My head gets so con - fused, hard to o - bey.
Chorus:
A5
C5
3
D5
5
F5
I kissed a girl and I liked it, the taste of her
E5
A5
C5
3
D5
5
cher - ry chap - stick. I kissed a girl just to try it.

F5
E5
A5
C5
I hope my boy - friend don't mind it.
It felt so wrong,
D5
F5
E5
A5
it felt so right, don't mean I'm in love to - night.
To Coda
C5
D5
F5
I kissed a girl and I liked it,
1.
E5
A5
N.C.
I liked it.
(Drums only)
2.
E5
I liked it.

Bridge:
F
Em
Am/E
Em7
Us girls, we are so mag - i - cal, soft skin, red lips, so kiss - a - ble.
F
Em
Am/E
Em7
Hard to re - sist, so touch - a - ble. Too good to de - ny it.
D.S. 𝄋 al Coda
Dm
Ain't no big deal, it's in - no - cent.
(Ooh.)
Coda
E5
A5
I liked it.
(Ooh.)

I TURN TO YOU

Words and Music by
DIANE WARREN

© 1996 REALSONGS (ASCAP)
All Rights Reserved

D♭
A♭/C
los - ing ground, when my
an - y - thing, coz your
*F♭maj9
E♭m7
world is go - ing cra - zy, you can turn it all a - round.
love is so a - maz - ing, coz your love in - spi - res me.
F7(♯5)
B♭m7
And when I'm down, you're there, push-ing me to the top.
And when I need a friend, you're al - ways on my side,
E♭m7
E♭m7/A♭
You're al - ways there giv - ing me all you've got.
giv - ing me faith, tak - ing me through the night.
For a shield

* F♭ = E

Chorus:
D♭
E♭m7
D♭/F
G♭maj7
from the storm, for a friend, for a love to keep me safe
E♭m7
E♭m7/A♭
and warm, I turn to you. For the strength
D♭
E♭m7
1.
D♭/F
C♭maj9
to be strong, for the will to car - ry on, for
E♭m7
A/B
E♭m7/A♭
ev - 'ry - thing you do, for ev - 'ry - thing that's true, I turn to you.

D♭
Amaj7/E
E♭m7
2. When I lose
2.
D♭/F
C♭maj9
to car - ry on,
for
E♭m7
D♭
ev - 'ry - thing you do, I turn to you.
Bridge:
C♭maj9
B♭m7
For the arms to be my shel - ter through all the rain,
for

A♭7sus
A♭m7/D♭ D♭ A♭m7/D♭ D♭
C♭maj9
truth that will nev-er change, for some - one to lean on, for a heart I can re -
G♭/B♭
E♭m7/A♭
ly on through an - y - thing, for that one who I can
run to, I turn to you.
For a shield
Chorus:
E♭
Fm7
E♭/G
A♭maj7
Fm7
from the storm, for a friend, for a love to keep me safe and warm, I

Fm7/B♭
E♭
Fm7
turn to you. For the strength to be strong, for the will
E♭/G
D♭maj9
Fm7
to car - ry on, for ev - 'ry - thing you do, for
C♭/D♭
Fm7/B♭
Fm7
ev - 'ry - thing that's true, for ev - 'ry - thing you do, for
C♭/D♭
Fm7/B♭
Freely
E♭
ev - 'ry - thing that's true, I turn to you.
rit.

IF EVERYONE CARED

Lyrics by
CHAD KROEGER

Music by
NICKELBACK

Gtr. in Drop D tuning:
⑥ = D ③ = G
⑤ = A ② = B
④ = D ① = E

© 2005 WARNER-TAMERLANE PUBLISHING CORP., ARM YOUR DILLO PUBLISHING, INC.,
ZERO-G MUSIC INC., BLACK DIESEL MUSIC INC. and DANIEL ADAIR PUBLISHING DESIGNEE
All Rights Administered by WARNER-TAMERLANE PUBLISHING CORP.
All Rights Reserved

A
E
F♯
"A - men, I, I'm a - live." Sing - ing,
p
A
E
F♯
"A - men, I, I'm a - live." If ev - 'ry - one cared
Chorus:
F♯5
C♯5
E5
F♯5
and no-bod - y cried, if ev - 'ry-one loved and no-bod - y lied. If ev - 'ry-one shared
f
1.
D5
A5
E5
and swal-lowed their pride, we'd see the day when no - bod - y died.

F♯5
A5
And I'm sing - ing, "A - a - men I, a - men, I,
E5
F♯5
F♯5
A5
I'm a - live." "A - men, I, a - men, I a - men, I,
E5
2.3.
D5
A5
I'm a-live." 2. And in the air and swal-lowed their pride, would we see the day
E5
F♯5
D5
A5
when no-bod-y died. If ev-'ry-one cared and no-bod-y cried, if ev-'ry-one loved

E5
F♯5
D5
A5
and no-bod-y lied. If ev-'ry-one shared and swal-lowed their pride, we'd see the day
To Coda
when no-bod-y died.
When no-bod-y died.
3. And as we lie
Verse 3:
F♯
A
E
F♯
be-neath the stars we re-al-ize how small we are. If they could love

A
E
F♯
D.S. 𝄋 al Coda
like you and me, i - mag - ine what the world could be. If ev-'ry-one cared
Coda
D5
A5
E5
(Would we see the day, would we see the day?)
When no-bod - y died.
D5
A5
E5
F♯5
(Would we see the day, would we see the day?)
When no-bod - y died.
D5
A5
E5
(Would we see the day?)
When no - bod - y died.

INSIDE YOUR HEAVEN

Words and Music by
ANDREAS CARLSSON, PER NYLEN
and SAVAN KOTECHA

© 2005 WB MUSIC CORP., ANDREAS CARLSSON PUBLISHING AB, UNIVERSAL MUSIC PUBLISHING AB and OH SUKI MUSIC
All Rights on behalf of itself and ANDREAS CARLSSON PUBLISHING AB Administered by WB MUSIC CORP.
All Rights Reserved

D
Dsus
D
Am7
G/B
C(9)
Dsus
D
The sun and the moon - light, all my dreams are in your eyes. And
Chorus:
G
C(9)
G/B
I wan - na be in - side your heav - en. Take me to the place you cry
Am7
G/B
C(9)
Dsus
D
G
from, where the storm blows your way. And I wan-na be the earth that holds
C(9)
G/B
Am7
G/B
you, ev - 'ry bit of air you're breath - in' in, a sooth - in' wind. I

C(9)
Dsus
D
G
G/B
C(9)
wan - na be in - side your heav - en.
2. When we
Verse 2:
G
C/G
G
touch, when we love, the stars line up, the wrong be - comes un - done.
C/G
D/F♯
Em
F
C
Am7
G/B
Nat - 'ral - ly, my soul sur - ren - ders. The sun and the moon - light, all my
C(9)
Dsus
D
Chorus:
G
C(9)
G/B
dreams are in your eyes. And I wan-na be in - side your heav - en. Take me to the place you cry

Am7 G/B C(9) Dsus D G
from, where the storm blows your way. And I wan-na be the earth that holds
C(9) G/B Am7 G/B
you, ev - 'ry bit of air you're breath - in' in, a sooth - in' wind. I
C(9) Dsus D G
wan - na be in - side your heav - en.
Bridge:
C(9) G/B
When min-utes turn to days and years, if
Am7 D C(9) G/B
moun-tains fall, I'll still be here hold - ing you un - til the day I die.

Chorus:
Dsus
N.C.
G
C(9)
G/B
I wan-na be in-side your heav - en. Take me to the place you cry
mp
Em
D
G/B
Am/C
Bm/D
C/E
D
G
from, where the storm blows your way.
(I wan-na be in-side your heav -
cresc.
mf
D.S. 𝄋 and fade
C(9)
G/B
Am7
G/B
C(9)
Dsus
D
en.)
I wan-na be in-side where the storm blows your way.

LEAVIN'

Words and Music by
TERIUS NASH, CORRON COLE, JAMES BUNTON
and CHRISTOPHER STEWART

© 2008 WB MUSIC CORP., 2082 MUSIC PUBLISHING, UNIVERSAL MUSIC-MGB SONGS,
HOLY CORRON MUSIC, MOVE JB SONGS, SONGS OF PEER LTD. and MARCHNINENTH MUSIC
All Rights on behalf of itself and 2082 MUSIC PUBLISHING Administered by WB MUSIC CORP.
All Rights Reserved

A
F♯m7
You make me wan - na take you out and let it rain, let it rain, let it rain, let it rain.
'Cause you're the bad - dest lit - tle thing that I've ev - er seen, ev - er seen, ev - er seen, ev - er seen.
E
Dmaj7
I know you got a man, but this is what you should say,
So, I'm - a ask you one time, if you got a man,
why don't you tell him that, "I'm
Chorus:
A
F♯m7
leav - in', nev - er to come back a - gain." You found some - bod - y who does it bet - ter than he can.
E
Dmaj7
No more mak - in' you cry, no more them gray skies. Girl, we fly - in' on the G 5, G 5, and we're

A
F♯m7
leav - in', nev - er to come back a - gain. So call your shor - ty and tell him you found a new man.
E
Dmaj7
The one that's so, so fly, the one that keep you high, have you sing - in' all night, like, like... Oh -
A
F♯m7
oh, oh, oh, oh. Oh - oh, oh, man, she's gon' be sing - in' oh -
To Coda
1.
2.
E
Dmaj7
Dmaj7
oh, oh, oh. Oh - oh, oh - oh. oh, oh - oh.

Bridge:
A
F♯m7
Don't stress, don't stress, don't stress, just tell him to the left, left,
E
Dmaj7
left. Don't stress, don't stress, don't stress, 'cause we gone and we gone and we gone.
A
F♯m7
No stress, no stress, no stress, girl, you de - serve noth - in' but the
E
Dmaj7
D.S. 𝄋 al Coda
best. No stress, no stress, no stress. Girl, you need to tell him that, "I'm

Coda
Dmaj7
A
oh, oh - oh. oh, oh, oh, oh. Oh -
F♯m7
E
oh, oh, man, she's gon' be sing - in' oh - oh, oh, oh. Oh -
Dmaj7
A
F♯m7
oh, oh - oh.
(Vocal ad lib.)
E
Dmaj7
Repeat ad lib. and fade
A
Optional ending

LIVE YOUR LIFE

Words and Music by
CLIFFORD HARRIS, MAKEBA RIDDICK,
JUSTIN SMITH and MIHAI BALAN DAN

© 2008 WARNER-TAMERLANE PUBLISHING CORP., CROWN CLUB PUBLISHING, YOGA FLAMES PUBLISHING,
FOB MUSIC PUBLISHING and EMI APRIL MUSIC INC.
All Rights on behalf of itself and CROWN CLUB PUBLISHING Administered by WARNER-TAMERLANE PUBLISHING CORP.
All Rights Reserved

mi - ya ha ha. Mi - ya hee, mi - ya ho, mi - ya hu,
is be thankful for the life you got, know what I'm saying?
Stop looking at what you ain't got and start being thankful for what you do got.
Chorus:
G
D
mi - ya ha ha. You're gon - na be a shin - ing star in fan - cy clothes
Let's give it to 'em, baby girl!
A
Bm
G
D
and fan - cy cars. And then you'll see you're gon - na go far, 'cause ev - 'ry - one knows
A
Bm
G
D
just who you are. So live your life, ay.

A
Bm
G
D
You stead - y chas - in' that pa - per. Just live your life, ay.
A
Bm
G
D
Ain't got no time for no hat - ers. Just live your life, ay.
A
Bm
G
D
No tell - in' where it will take ya. Just live your life, ay.
A
Bm
G
D
'Cause I'm a pa - per chas - er, just liv - in' my life, my life, my life,

A
Bm
G
D
To Coda
my life. Just liv - in' my life, my life, my life,
A
Bm
Verse:
N.C.
my life. Just liv - in' my life.
1. Never mind what haters say, ignore them 'til they fade away.
2. See additional lyrics
Amazing they ungrateful after all the game I gave away.
Safe to say I paved the way for you cats to get paid today.
You'd still be wasting days away now had I never saved the day.
Consider them my protégé, homage I think they should pay.

Instead of being gracious, they violate in a major way.
I never been a hater, still I love them in a crazy way.
G
D
Some say they sold the yay and know they couldn't get work on Labor Day. It ain't that black and white, it has an area the shade of gray.
A
Bm
G
D
I'm Westside anyway, even if I left today and stayed away.
Some move away to make a way, not move away 'cause they afraid.
A
Bm
G
D
I brought back to the hood and all you ever did was take away.
I pray for patience, but they make me wanna melt their face away.

A
Bm
G
D
Like I once made them spray, now I could make them put the K's away.
Been thuggin' all my life, can't say I don't deserve to take a break.
1.
2.
D.S. 𝄋 al Coda
You're gon - na be
You'd rather see me catch a case and watch my future fade away.
And we mighty full of ourselves all of a sudden, aren't we?
Coda
my life. Got ev - 'ry - bod - y watch - in' what I do. Come walk in my shoes and
see the way I'm liv - ing, if you real - ly want to. Got my mind on my mon - ey and I'm not go - in' a - way.

A
Bm
G
D
So, keep on get - tin' your pa - per and keep on climb - in'. Look in the mir -
ror and keep on shin - in'. Till the game end, till the clock stop, we gon'
post up on the top spot. Liv - in' the life, the life, in a
brand - new cit - y, got my whole team with me. The life, the life, I

A
Bm
G
D
do it how I wan-na do. I'm liv-in' my life, my life,
A
Bm
G
D
I will nev-er lose, I'm liv-in' my life, my life, and
A
Bm
G
D
I'm not stop-ping. Mi-ya hee, mi-ya ho, mi-ya hu,
A
Bm
G
D
mi-ya ha ha. Mi-ya hee, mi-ya ho, mi-ya hu,

Verse 2:
I'm the opposite of moderate, immaculately polished with
The spirit of a hustler and the swagger of a college kid.
Allergic to the counterfeit, impartial to the politics,
*Articulate, but still I'll grab a n***** by the collar quick.*

Whoever having problems with their record sales just holla till.
If that don't work and all else fails, then turn around and follow till.
I got love for the game but, ay, I'm not in love with all of it.
'Could do without the fame and the rappers nowadays are comedy.

The hootin' and the hollerin', back and forth with the arguing,
Where you from, who you know, what you make, and what kind of car you in.
Seems as though you lost sight of what's important when depositin'
Them checks into your bank account and you up out of poverty.

Your values is a disarray, prioritizing horribly,
Unhappy with your riches 'cause you're piss-poor morally,
Ignoring all prior advice and forewarning.
And we mighty full of ourselves all of a sudden, aren't we?
(To Chorus:)

MY IMMORTAL

Words and Music by
BEN MOODY, AMY LEE
and DAVID HODGES

© 2003 FSMGI (IMRO), ZOMBIES ATE MY PUBLISHING (BMI) and FORTHEFALLEN PUBLISHING (BMI)
All Rights Administered by STATE ONE MUSIC AMERICA (BMI)
All Rights Reserved

C♯m
A(9)
I wish that you would just leave, 'cause your pre-sence still lin - gers here,
C♯m
F♯m
C♯m
4fr.
and it won't leave me a - lone. These wounds won't seem to heal.
F♯m
C♯m
4fr.
F♯m
C♯m
4fr.
E
Esus
E
This pain is just too real. There's just too much that time can - not e - rase.
Chorus:
F♯m
E /D
Esus/D
E
C♯m
4fr.
When you cried, I'd wipe a - way all of your tears.

F♯m
E /D
Esus/D
E
C♯m
4fr.
When you'd scream, I'd fight a - way all of your fears.
F♯m
E /D
Esus/D
E
C♯m
4fr.
F♯m
E /D
Esus/D
And I've held your hand through all of these years, but you still
To Coda
1.
E
A
have all of me.
C♯m
A(9)
C♯m

Bridge:
2.
D(9)
F♯m
C♯m
4fr.
all of me.
I've tried so hard to tell my - self that you're
D
Bm9
C♯m
4fr.
gone. And though you're still with me,
E /D
D
E
Esus
F♯m
D
I've been a - lone all a - long.
D.S. 𝄋 al Coda
E
C♯m
4fr.
F♯m
D
E
C♯m
4fr.

Verse 2:
You used to captivate me
By your resonating light.
But, now I'm bound by the life you left behind.
Your face, it haunts
My once pleasant dreams.
Your voice, it chased away
All the sanity in me.
These wounds won't seem to heal.
This pain is just too real.
There's just too much that time can not erase.
(To Chorus:)

MY LIFE WOULD SUCK WITHOUT YOU

Words and Music by
CLAUDE KELLY, LUKASZ GOTTWALD
and MAX MARTIN

© 2008 WARNER-TAMERLANE PUBLISHING CORP., STUDIO BEAST MUSIC, KASZ MONEY PUBLISHING and KOBALT SONGS MUSIC PUBLISHING
All Rights on behalf of itself and STUDIO BEAST MUSIC Administered by WARNER-TAMERLANE PUBLISHING CORP.
All Rights Reserved

D
A
ry. You're stand - ing at my door.
pid for tell - ing you good - bye.
C♯m
F♯m
D
Guess this means you take back all you said be - fore,
May - be I was wrong for try'n' to pick a fight.
E
A
like how much you want - ed
I know that I've got is - sues, but you're
D
A
C♯m
an - y - one but me. Said you'd nev - er come
pret - ty messed up too. Ei - ther way, I found

F♯m
D
E
back, but here you are a - gain.
out I'm noth - ing with - out you.
Chorus:
Esus
N.C.
A
F♯m7
'Cause we be - long to - geth - er now,
f
Dmaj7
E
A
yeah. For - ev - er u - nit - ed here
F♯m7
C♯m
E
some - how, yeah. You got a piece

A
F♯m7
Bm
of me,
and, hon - est - ly,
D
A
F♯m7
my life (my life) would suck (would suck) with - out
Dmaj9
1.
Esus
E
2.
Esus
E
you.
Verse 3:
A
D
3. Be - ing with you is so dys - func - tion - al.
mp

A
C♯m
F♯m
I real - ly should - n't miss you, but
D
E
A
I can't let you go, oh, yeah. (Inst. solo ad lib....
D
A
C♯m
F♯m
D

Esus
E
Esus
N.C.
...end solo)
'Cause we be - long
Chorus:
A
F♯m7
Dmaj7
to - geth - er now,
yeah.
E
A
F♯m7
For - ev - er u - nit - ed here
some - how,
C♯m
E
A
yeah.
You got a piece
of me,

F♯m7
Bm
D
and, hon - est - ly, my life
A
F♯m7
(my life) would suck (would suck) with - out
1.
Dmaj9
Esus
you. 'Cause we be - long
2.
Esus
A

NEW SOUL

Words and Music by
YAEL NAIM and DAVID DONATIEN

© 2007 LILI LOUISE MUSIQUE SARL (SACEM)
All Rights Administered by WB MUSIC CORP. (ASCAP)
All Rights Reserved

Chorus:
F
Am
G
la la, la la la la la la, la la la la la, la la la, la la
C
F
la. La la la la, la la la la la la, la la la la
Am
G
1.
C
2.
C
la, la la la, la la la. 2. See I'm a la. Ooh.
F
Am
G

C
F
Bridge:
Am
G
C
Gm
This is a hap - py end,
C
F
Fm
'cause you don't un - der-stand
Gm
C
F
ev - 'ry-thing you have done.
Now why's ev - 'ry - thing so wrong?

Fm
Gm
C
This is a hap - py end.
Come and give me your hand.
Verse 3:
F
Fm
C
I'll take you far
a - way.
3. I'm a new soul, I came to this
F
Em
G
strange world hop - ing I could learn a bit 'bout how to give and take.
But since I
C
F
Am
G
came here, felt the joy and the fear, find - ing my - self mak - ing ev - 'ry pos - si - ble mis -

C
F
take. A new soul in this ver - y
(La la la la, la la la la la la, la la la la
Am
G
C
strange world. Mak - ing ev - 'ry pos - si - ble
la, la la la, la la la. La la la la, la la la la
F
Em
G
mis - take, pos - si - ble mis - take, ev - 'ry...
la la, la la la la la, la la la, la la la. La la
(Lead Vocal ad lib....
F
Em
G
la la la la la la la la las la la la la la la la la la. La la

C
F
Em
G
Ia la la la la la la la la la la la la la la la la la la la la la la la.
A little slower
C
F
Em
G
Ah, ah.
C
F
Em
G
Ah, ah.
C
F
C
G
Ah, ah.

ONE STEP AT A TIME

Words and Music by
MICH HANSEN, JONAS JEBERG,
ROBBIE NEVIL and LAUREN EVANS

*Original recording in D♭ major.

© 2007 CUTFATHER PUBLISHING LIMITED, MURLYN SONGS AB, LAUREN CROWN MUSIC and Z STYLE MUSIC
All Rights in the U.S. and Canada for CUTFATHER PUBLISHING LIMITED
Administered by WARNER-TAMERLANE PUBLISHING CORP.
All Rights Reserved

Em
D
Bm
A
So close, but so far a - way.
You're con - fused and got it all fig - ured out.
Em
D
Bm
A
Ev - 'ry - thing that you al - ways dreamed of,
Ev - 'ry - thing that you al - ways wished for
G
A
close e - nough for you to taste, but you just can't touch.
could be yours, should be yours, would be yours if they on - ly knew.
Em
D
You wan - na show the world, but no one knows your name yet.

Bm
A
You won - der when and where and how you're gon - na make it.
Em
D
Bm
A
You know_ you can, if you get__ the chance, in your face and the door keeps slam - ing.__
Em
D
Bm
A
Now you're feel - ing more and more frus - tra - ted, and you're get - ting all kind of im - pa - tient,
G
A
wait - in'. We live and we learn____ to take one

Chorus:
Em D Bm A Em D
step at a time. There's no need to rush. It's like learn-ing to fly or
mf
Bm A Em D Bm A
fall-ing in love. It's gon-na hap-pen and it's sup-posed to hap-pen that we
G 1. A Em D
find the rea - sons why, one step at a time. Da da da da da da
Bm A Em D Bm A
da da da da n da da. Da da da da da da da da da da n da da.

2.
Bridge:
A
Cmaj9
Fmaj7
one step at a time.
When you can't wait an - y long - er,
(You
Cmaj9
Fmaj7
but there's no end in sight.
can't wait.)
(When you
Dmaj7
Gmaj9
3
It's your faith that makes you strong - er.
need to find the strengh.)
(The
Asus
F♯m7/B
A/C♯
D
Em
D
The on - ly way we get there is one step at a time.
on - ly way we get there.)
mp

Bm A Em D Bm A
Da da da da da da da da da da n da da.
Take one
Chorus:
Em D Bm A Em D
step at a time. There's no need to rush. It's like learn-ing to fly or
mf
Bm A Em D Bm A
fall-ing in love. It's gon-na hap-pen and it's sup-posed to hap-pen that we
G 1. A 2. A D5
find the rea - sons why, one step at a time. one step at a time.
One

PARTY IN THE U.S.A.

Words and Music by
CLAUDE KELLY, LUKASZ GOTTWALD
and JESSICA CORNISH

*Recording in F♯ major.

© 2009 WARNER-TAMERLANE PUBLISHING CORP., STUDIO BEAST MUSIC, KASZ MONEY PUBLISHING and JESSICA CORNISH PUBLISHING DESIGNEE
All Rights on behalf of itself and STUDIO BEAST MUSIC Administered by WARNER-TAMERLANE PUBLISHING CORP.
All Rights Reserved

F Am Dm C
Wel - come to the land of fame ex - cess. Am I gon - na fit in?
"Who's that chick that's rock - in' Kicks. She's got - ta be from out of town."
F Am Dm C
Jumped in the cab, here I am for the first time. Look to my right, and I see the Hol - ly - wood sign.
So hard with my girls not a - round me. It's def - i - nite-ly not a Nash - ville par - ty,
F Am Dm C
This is all so cra - zy. Ev - 'ry - bod - y seems so fa - mous.
'cause all I see are sti - let - tos. I guess I nev - er got the mem - o.
F Am Dm C
My tum-my's turn-ing and I'm feel-ing kind of home-sick. Too much pres-sure and I'm ner-vous. That's when the
My tum-my's turn-ing and I'm feel-ing kind of home-sick. Too much pres-sure and I'm ner-vous. That's when the

F
Am
Dm
C
tax - i - man turned on the ra - di - o and a Jay - Z song was on, and a
D J dropped my fa - v'rite tune and a Brit - ney song was on, and a
N.C.
Jay - Z song was on, and a Jay - Z song was on.
Brit - ney song was on, and a Brit - ney song was on.
So, I put my
Chorus:
F
Am
Dm
C
hands up, they're play - ing my song. The but - ter - flies fly a - way.
F
Am
Dm
C
Nod-ding my head, like, yeah. Mov - ing my hips, like, yeah. I got my

F
Am
Dm
C
hands up, they're play - ing my song. I know I'm gon - na be o - kay.
Yeah, it's a par - ty in the U. S. A.
1.
2.
Yeah, it's a par-ty in the U. S. A. par-ty in the U. S. A.
Bridge:
Feel like hop - ping on a flight
(On a flight.)

Am
Gm
back to my home - town to - night.
(Town to - night.)
Am
Dm
Some-thing stops me ev - 'ry time,
(Ev - 'ry time.)
the
B♭
C
D J plays my song and I feel al - right.
(Right.)
So I put my
Chorus:
F
Am
Dm
C
hands up, they're play - ing my song. The but - ter - flies fly a - way.

F
Am
Dm
C
Nod-ding my head, like, yeah. Mov-ing my hips, like, yeah. I got my
hands up, they're play - ing my song. I know I'm gon - na be o - kay.
Yeah, it's a par - ty in the U. S. A.
1.
2.
F5
Yeah, it's a par-ty in the U. S. A. Gon-na put my par-ty in the U. S. A.

Gtr. tuned down 1/2 step:
⑥ = E♭ ③ = G♭
⑤ = A♭ ② = B♭
④ = D♭ ① = E♭

PHOTOGRAPH

Lyrics by
CHAD KROEGER

Music by
NICKELBACK

Moderately slow ♩ = 76

Verse:

Guitar → *E5* — E♭5 — *B(4)* — B♭(4)

Piano →

1. Look at this pho - to - graph, ev - 'ry time I do, it makes me laugh.

mf

D6/9 — D♭6/9 — *A(9)* — A♭(9)

How did our eyes get so red? And what the hell is on Jo - ey's head?

E5 — E♭5 — *B(4)* — B♭(4)

And this is where I grew up, I think the pres-ent own-er fixed it up.
2. Re-mem-ber the old ar - cade? Blew ev - 'ry dol - lar that we ev - er made.

© 2005 WARNER-TAMERLANE PUBLISHING CORP., ARM YOUR DILLO PUBLISHING, INC.,
ZERO-G MUSIC INC., BLACK DIESEL MUSIC INC. and DANIEL ADAIR PUBLISHING DESIGNEE
All Rights Administered by WARNER-TAMERLANE PUBLISHING CORP.
All Rights Reserved

Photograph - 6 - 2

D6/9
D♭6/9
A(9)
A♭(9)
Life's bet - ter now than it was back then, if I was them, I would-n't let me in.
She's had a cou - ple of kids since then, I have-n't seen her since God knows when.
G6
G♭6
A(9)
A♭(9)
Oh, whoa, whoa, oh, God, I, I. Ev - 'ry
Chorus:
E5
E♭5
B(4)
B♭(4)
mem-o - ry of look-ing out the back door, I had the pho - to al - bum spread out on the bed - room floor. It's
D6/9
D♭6/9
A(9)
A♭(9)
hard to say it, time to say it, good - bye, good - bye. Ev - 'ry

Photograph - 6 - 4

A(9)
5
A♭(9)
E5
7
E♭5
you can't re - place it. I miss it now,
B(4)
7
B♭(4)
G6
3
G♭6
I can't be - lieve it. So hard to stay,
A(9)
5
A♭(9)
E5
7
E♭5
too hard to leave it. If I could re - live those days,
B(4)
7
B♭(4)
D6/9
10
D♭6/9
D.S. 𝄋 al Coda
I know the one thing that would nev - er change.
Ev - 'ry

Coda
A(9)
A♭(9)
E5
E♭5
good - bye, good - bye.
Look at this pho - to - graph.
B(4)
B♭(4)
D6/9
D♭6/9
A(9)
A♭(9)
Ev-'ry time I do, it makes me laugh.
Ev-'ry time I do, it makes me...

SMILE

Words and Music by
MATTHEW SHAFER, BLAIR DALY,
J.T. HARDING and JEREMY BOSE

© 2009 WARNER-TAMERLANE PUBLISHING CORP., GAJE MUSIC, INC., SONGS OF WINDSWEPT PACIFIC,
MUSIC OF COMBUSTION, BLESS THE BIKINI MUSIC, JTX MUSIC and VANDELAY PUBLISHING
All Rights on behalf of itself and GAJE MUSIC, INC. Administered by WARNER-TAMERLANE PUBLISHING CORP.
All Rights Reserved

Verses 1 (cont.) & 2:
E
F♯m9
Amaj9
(1.) Com-plete-ly un - a - ware, noth-ing can com-pare to where you send
2. E - ven when you're gone, some-how you come a - long just like a flow-
B
A
F♯m7(4)
A
me, lets me know that it's o - kay. yeah, it's o - kay, in the
er pok - ing through the side - walk crack, and just like that, you
mf
B
A
F♯m7(4)
N.C.
mo-ments when my good times start to fade.
steal a - way the rain, and just like that...
You make me smile
Chorus:
E
B
A
F♯m7
like the sun, fall out of bed, sing like a bird, diz - zy in my head, spin
f

E
B
A
F♯m7
like a rec-ord, cra - zy on a Sun - day night.
You make me dance
E
B
C♯m7
A
like a fool, for - get how to breathe, shine like gold, buzz like a bee.
1.
E
B
A
F♯m7
N.C.
Just the thought of you can drive me wild.
Oh, you make me
E
F♯m9
Amaj9
smile.
mp

2.
Bridge:
A
F♯m7
C♯m
C♯m7/B
wild. Oh, you make me smile.
Don't know how I live with-out you,
F♯9/A♯
C♯m
C♯m7/B
'cause ev-'ry time that I get a-round you
I see the best of me in-side your eyes.
F♯9/A♯
Amaj9
You make me smile.
B
E
F♯m9
You make me dance like a fool, for-get how to breathe, shine
mp

Amaj9
E
F♯m9
like gold, buzz like a bee. Just the thought of you can drive me wild.
Chorus:
Amaj9
E
B
You make me smile like the sun, fall out of bed, sing
f
A
F♯m7
E
B
like a bird, diz - zy in my head, spin like a rec-ord, cra - zy on a Sun - day night.
A
F♯m7
E
B
You make me dance like a fool, for - get how to breathe, shine

C♯m7
A
E
B
like gold, buzz like a bee. Just the thought of you can drive me
A
F♯m7
E
F♯m9
wild. Oh, you make me smile.
Oh, you make me
mf
Amaj9
E
F♯m9
Oh, you make me smile.
smile.
Oh, you make me
Amaj9
N.C.
Oh, you make me smile.
smile.

SOAK UP THE SUN

Words and Music by
SHERYL CROW and JEFF TROTT

© 2002 FSMGI (IMRO) and CYRILLIC SOUP
All Rights for FSMGI (IMRO) Administered by STATE ONE MUSIC AMERICA (BMI)
All Rights Reserved

1.
A(9)
E
B5
A(9)
his gas.
So I'm stuck here watch - ing T V.
you want.
It's want - ing what
2.
E
B5
A(9)
A(9)
you've got.
Chorus:
E
B
I'm gon - na soak up the sun,
F♯m
A
I'm gon - na tell ev - 'ry - one to light - en

B
E
up.
(I'm gon - na tell 'em that)
I've
B
got no one to blame.
For ev - 'ry time I feel
F♯m
A
B
lame I'm look - ing up.
E
B5
A(9)
I'm gon - na soak up the sun
I'm gon - na soak up the

Verses 3 & 4:
E
B5
A(9)
E
B5
sun.
3. I've got a crum -
4. Don't have no mas -
A(9)
E
B5
A(9)
my job.
It don't pay near e - nough
ter suite,
but I'm still the king of me.
E
B5
A(9)
E
B5
to buy the things it takes
to win me some
You have a fan - cy ride, but ba - by,
I'm the one who has
Bridge:
A(9)
E
E/D♯
D(9)
A/C♯
of your love.
the key.
Ev - 'ry time I turn a - round, I'm look - ing up, you're look - ing down.

Second time only
E
E/D♯
G
A
G
A
May - be some - thing's wrong with you that makes you act the way you do.
May - be I am cra - zy too.
Chorus:
E
B
I'm gon - na soak up the sun,
F♯m
A
I'm gon - na tell ev - 'ry - one to light - en
B
E
up.
(I'm gon - na tell 'em that)
I've

B
got no one to blame.
For ev - 'ry time I feel
F♯m
A
B
To Coda
lame I'm look - ing up.
E
B5
A(9)
I'm gon - na soak up the sun
while it's still
E
B5
A(9)
E
B5
free.
I'm gon - na soak up the sun

D.S. 𝄋 al Coda
A(9)
E
B5
A(9)
be - fore it goes out on me.
Coda
E
B
I'm gon - na soak up the sun,
F♯m
A
B
I've got my for - ty - five on so I can rock on.
rit.

STICKWITU

Words and Music by
FRANNE GOLDE, ROBERT PALMER
and KASIA LIVINGSTON

© 2005 FRANNE GEE MUSIC, SONY/ATV MUSIC PUBLISHING UK LTD., PARCHI MUSIC,
KOALA BEAR MUSIC LTD and DAD'S DREAMER
All Rights for FRANNE GEE MUSIC Administered by WARNER-TAMERLANE PUBLISHING CORP.
All Rights Reserved

D
A(9)/C♯
Bm7
A7
Bm7
A/C♯
ev - 'ry - bod - y's break-in' up___ and throw-in' their love a - way.___ But I
D
A(9)/C♯
Bm7
A(9)
know I got a good thing right_ here. That's why_ I say... Hey,___
Chorus:
D
A(9)/C♯
Bm7
A7
Bm7
A/C♯
___ no - bod - y gon - na love me bet - ter, I'm - a___ stick with you for - ev - er.
D
A(9)/C♯
Bm7
A(9)
No - bod - y gon - na take me high - er, I'm - a___ stick with you.

1.
D
A(9)/C♯
Bm7
A7
Bm7
A/C♯
You know_ how to 'pre - ci - ate me, I'm - a___ stick with you, my__ ba - by.___
D
A(9)/C♯
Bm7
A(9)
___ No - bod - y ev - er made me feel this way. I'm - a___ stick with you.___
2.
D
Bm7
C♯m7
F♯m7
You know_ how to 'pre - ci - ate me, I'm - a___ stick with you, my__ ba - by.___
D
A(9)/C♯
Bm7
A(9)
___ No - bod - y ev - er made me feel this way. I'm - a___ stick with you.___ And

256
Bridge:
Dmaj9
C♯m7
F♯m7
there ain't noth - in' else I could need. And
(Noth-in' else I could need.)
Dmaj9
C♯m7
F♯m7
I, I'm sing - ing 'cause you're so, so in - to me. I got you,
Dmaj9
C♯7
F♯m7
we'll be mak - in' love end - less - ly. I'm
Bm7
Bm7/E
with you, ba - by, you're with me.
(Ba - by, I'm with you.)
(Ba - by, you're with me, ah
sfz
sfz

Verse 3:
D(9)
A(9)/C♯
Bm7
A(9)
3. So, don't you wor-ry a-bout peo-ple hang-in' a-round. They ain't bring-in' us down. I
yeah.)
know you and you know me and that's all that counts.
So don't be wor-ried a-bout peo-ple hang-in' a-round. They ain't bring-in' us down. I
know you and you know me and that's, that's why I say... Hey,

Chorus:
D
A(9)/C♯
Bm7
A7
Bm7
A/C♯
no - bod - y gon - na love me bet - ter,
I'm - a stick with you for - ev - er.
D
A(9)/C♯
Bm7
A(9)
No - bod - y gon - na take me high - er,
I'm - a stick with you.
1.
D
A(9)/C♯
Bm7
A7
Bm7
A/C♯
You know how to 'pre - ci - ate me,
I'm - a stick with you, my ba - by.
D
A(9)/C♯
Bm7
A(9)
No - bod - y ev - er made me feel this way. I'm - a stick with you.

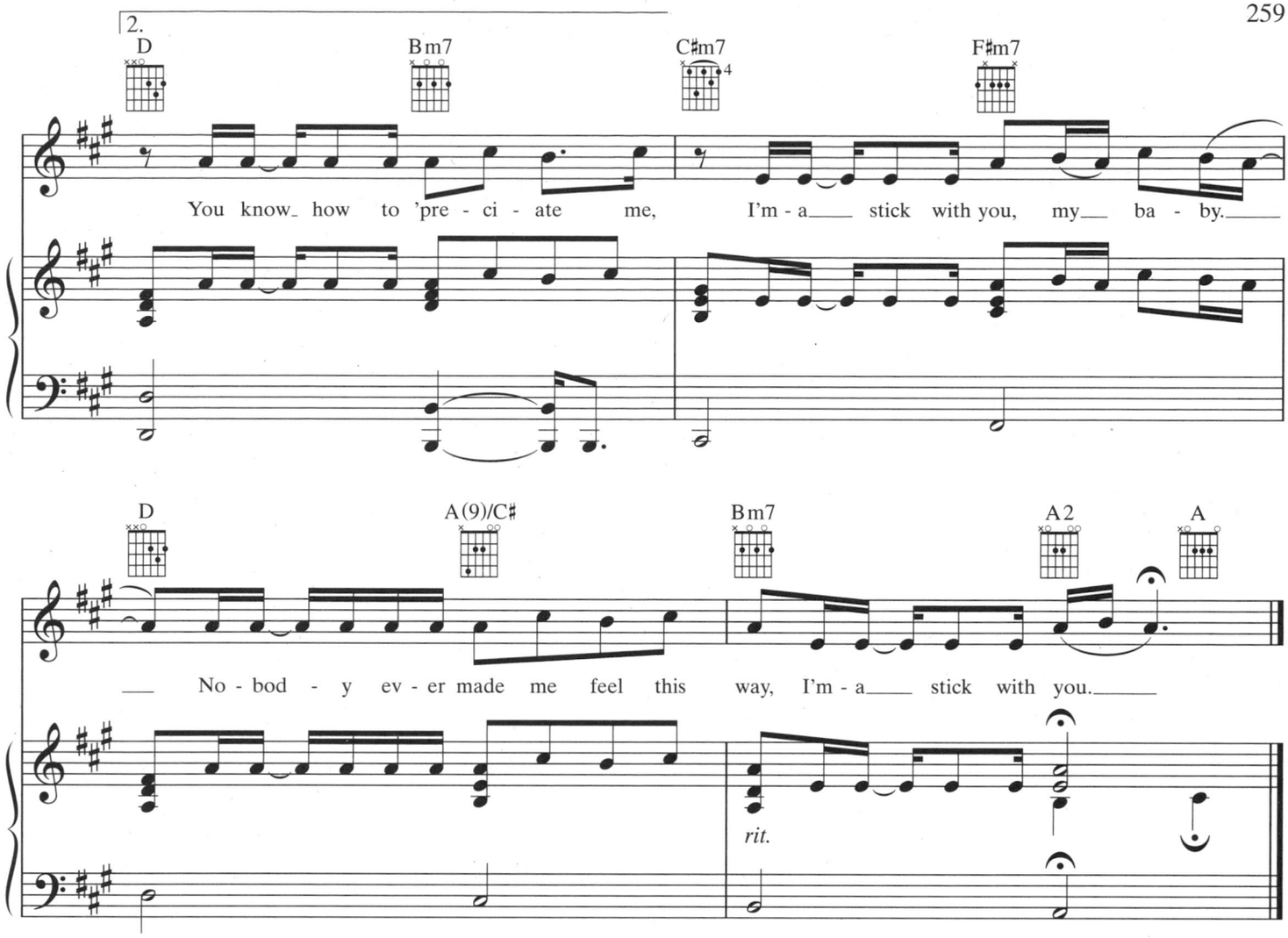

Verse 2:
I don't want to go another day,
So, I'm telling you exactly what is on my mind.
See, the way we ride in our private lives,
Ain't nobody getting in between.
I want you to know that you're the only one for me.
And I say…
(To Chorus:)

THE STORY

Words and Music by
PHIL HANSEROTH

*Original recording in B major, with guitar tuned down a half step.

© 2008 VIPER STRIKETH MUSIC
All Rights Administered by WB MUSIC CORP.
All Rights Reserved

F(9)
C
to where I am.
But these sto - ries don't mean
G7
Am
F(9)
an - y - thing
when you've got no one
to tell them to.
It's
C
G7
C
F/C
C
true,
I was made for you.
2. I climbed a - cross
Verses 2 & 3:
G7
the moun - tain tops,
swam all a - cross
the o - cean blue.
3. (Inst. solo ad lib....
f

Am
I crossed all the lines, and I broke all the rules, but, ba - by, I broke
F(9)
C
them all for you. Oh, be-cause e - ven when I was
G7
Am
F(9)
flat broke, you made me feel like a mil - lion bucks. You
C
Csus
G7
C
Csus
1.
C
do. I was made for you.

2.
Verse 4:
C
4. You see the smile that's on my mouth? It's hid - ing the words
...end solo)
mp
G7
Am
that don't come out. All of my friends who think that I'm blessed,
F(9)
they don't know my head is a mess. No,
C
G7
Am
they don't know who I real - ly am. And they don't know what I've
mf

F(9)
C
G7
been through like you do. And I was made for you.
C
F/C
C
Verse 5:
5. All of these lines a - cross my face
f
G7
tell you the sto - ry of who I am. So man - y sto -
Am
F(9)
ries of where I've been and how I got to where I am.

C
G7
Oh, but these sto-ries don't mean an-y-thing when you've
Am
F(9)
C
Csus
got no one to tell them to. It's true,
G7
C
Csus
C
Csus
I was made for you.
Oh, yeah, well, it's
C
Csus
G7
C
F/C
C
true that I was made for you.
mf
rit.

THIS IS IT

Written and Composed by
MICHAEL JACKSON
and PAUL ANKA

© 2009 MIJAC MUSIC (BMI) and PAULANNE MUSIC, INC. (BMI)
All Rights for MIJAC MUSIC (BMI) Administered by WARNER-TAMERLANE PUBLISHING CORP. (BMI)
All Rights Reserved

B♭
E♭/B♭
I can feel, and I know,
this is real, ev - 'ry time
we can sing, and I tell
B♭
E♭/B♭
yes, for sure, it is real. And it feels
I'm in love then I feel. And I feel
you I feel that way. And I feel
A♭/B♭
B♭
as though I've seen your face a thou - sand times, and you said
as though I've known you since a thou - sand years, and you tell
as though I've known you for a thou - sand years, and you're say -
A♭/B♭
B♭
you real - ly know me, too, your - self. And I know
me that you've seen my face be - fore. And you said
in' you want some of this your - self. And you said,

A♭/B♭
B♭
that you have got ad - dict - ed with your eyes, but you say
to me you don't want me hang - in' 'round man - y times;
"Won't you go with me on a walk?" And I know
A♭/B♭
B♭
you gon - na leave it for your - self, oh.
wan - na do it here be - fore, oh, yeah.
that it's real - ly for your - self, oh, yeah.
Bridge:
Cm7/B♭
B♭maj9
Cm7/B♭
I nev - er heard a sin - gle word a - bout you. Fall - ing in love was - n't my
mf
B♭maj9
Cm7/B♭
B♭maj9
plan. I nev - er thought that I would be your lov - er.

1.2.
3.
Cm7/B♭
B♭maj9
B♭maj9
Come on, ba - by, just un - der - stand.
2. This is it,
3. This is it,
stand.
mp
Bridge:
Cm7/B♭
B♭maj9
Cm7/B♭
I nev - er heard a sin - gle word a - bout you.
Fall - ing in love was - n't my
B♭maj9
Cm7/B♭
plan.
I nev - er thought that I would
B♭maj9
Cm7/B♭
B♭maj9
Repeat ad lib. and fade
be your lov - er.
Come on, ba - by, just un - der - stand.

UMBRELLA

Words and Music by
TERIUS NASH, SHAWN CARTER,
THADDIS HARRELL and
CHRISTOPHER STEWART

© 2007 2082 MUSIC PUBLISHING, EMI APRIL MUSIC, INC., CARTER BOYS MUSIC, SONGS OF PEER LTD.,
MARCH NINTH MUSIC PUBLISHING and MOBETTER GROOVES MUSIC
All Rights for 2082 MUSIC PUBLISHING Administered by WB MUSIC CORP.
All Rights Reserved

Verse:
G♭
D♭/A♭
had my heart and we'll nev - er be worlds a - part. May be in
fan - cy things will nev - er come in be - tween. You're part of my
Fm
B♭m
mag - a - zines, but you'll still be my star. Ba - by, 'cause
en - ti - ty, here for in - fin - i - ty. When the world has
G♭
D♭/A♭
in the dark, you can't see shin - y cars, and that's when you
took its part, when the world has dealt its cards, if the
Fm
B♭m
need me there. With you I'll al-ways share.
hand is hard, to - geth-er, we'll mend your heart. Be - cause,

Chorus:
G♭
D♭
when the sun shines, we'll shine to - geth - er. Told you I'll be here for - ev -
A♭
B♭m
er. Said I'll al - ways be your friend. Took an oath, I'm - a stick it out 'til the end.
G♭
D♭
Now that it's rain - in' more than ev - er, know that we'll still have each oth -
A♭
B♭m
er. You can stand un - der my um - br - el - la. You can stand un - der my um - br - el -

G♭
D♭/A♭
Fsus
la, el - la, el - la, eh, eh, eh. Un-der my um - br - el - la, el - la, el - la, eh,
B♭m
G♭
D♭/A♭
eh, eh. Un-der my um - br - el - la, el - la, el - la, eh, eh, eh. Un-der my um - br - el -
Fsus
1.
B♭m
2.
B♭m
la, el - la, el - la, eh, eh, eh, eh, eh, eh. eh, eh, eh, eh, eh.
2. These
Bridge:
C♭
G♭
You can run in - to my arms. It's o - kay, don't be a - larmed. Come

D♭
A♭5
B♭5
C♭
in - to me.
There's no dis - tance in be - tween our love.
So, I'm gon - na let the rain
G♭
F
pour. I'll be all you need and more.
Be - cause,
Chorus:
G♭
D♭/A♭
when the sun shines, we'll shine to - geth - er. Told you I'll be here for - ev -
F7
B♭m
er. Said I'll al - ways be your friend. Took an oath, I'm - a stick it out 'til the end.

G♭
D♭/A♭
Now that it's rain - in' more than ev - er, know that we'll still have each oth -
F7
B♭m
er. You can stand un - der my um - br - el - la. You can stand un - der my um - br - el -
G♭
D♭
la, el - la, el - la, eh, eh, eh. Un - der my um - br - el -
A♭
B♭m
la, el - la, el - la, eh, eh, eh. Un - der my um - br - el -

G♭
D♭
la, el - la, el - la, eh, eh, eh. Un - der my um - br - el -
A♭
B♭
la, el - la, el - la, eh, eh, eh, eh, eh. It's
G♭
D♭
rain - in', rain - in', ooh, ba - by, it's rain - in', rain - in'. Ba - by, come
A♭
B♭m
Repeat ad lib. and fade
in - to me, come in - to me. It's

WE BELONG TOGETHER

Words and Music by
KENNETH EDMONDS, DARNELL BRISTOL, SIDNEY JOHNSON,
JOHNTA AUSTIN, JERMAINE DUPRI, MANUEL SEAL, SANDRA SULLY,
MARIAH CAREY, PATRICK MOTEN and BOBBY WOMACK

© 2005 WARNER-TAMERLANE PUBLISHING CORP., EPIC/SOLAR SONGS, INC., HIP CHIC MUSIC, SONY SONGS INC.,
MISTER JOHNSONS JAMS MUSIC, CHRYSALIS MUSIC, NAKED UNDER MY CLOTHES MUSIC, EMI APRIL MUSIC INC., SHANIAH CYMONE MUSIC,
BMG SONGS, INC., SLACK AD MUSIC, BALLADS BY DESIGN, RYE SONGS and ABKCO MUSIC, INC., 85 Fifth Avenue, New York, NY 10003
{This song contains elements of ***"Two Occasions,"*** by Kenneth Edmonds, Darnell Bristol and Sidney Johnson, © 1997 Warner-Tamerlane Publishing Corp., Hip Chic Music, Epic/Solar Songs, Inc.,
Sony Songs Inc. and Splash Down Music and ***"If You Think You're Lonely Now,"*** by Bobby Womack, © 1981 Abkco Music, Inc., 85 Fifth Avenue, New York, NY 10003}
All Rights Reserved Used by Permission

Verse 1:

Fmaj7
G
Em7
F
1. I did-n't mean it when I said I did-n't love you so.
I should have held on tight, I nev-er should have let you go.
Fmaj7
G
Em7
Fmaj7
I did-n't know noth-ing, I was stu-pid, I was fool-ish, I was ly-in' to my - self.
G
Em7
F
I could-n't have fath-omed I would ev-er be with-out your love.
Nev-er i-mag-ined I'd be sit-ting here be-side my-self.
Fmaj7
G
Em7
Fmaj7
Guess I did-n't know you, 'cause I did-n't know me, but I thought I knew ev-'ry-thing.
I nev-er felt

G
Em7
Fmaj9
the feel-ing that I'm feel-ing now that I don't hear your voice, or have your touch or kiss your lips, 'cause I don't have a choice.
G
Em7
F
Oh, what I would-n't give to have you ly - in' by my side, right here, 'cause, ba - by,
Chorus:
Fmaj7
G
Em7
Fmaj9
when you left, I lost a part of me. It's still so hard to be -
G
Em7
F
lieve. Come back, ba - by, please 'cause we be - long to - geth - er. Who else am I gon'

Fmaj7
G
Em7
Fmaj9
lean on when times get rough? Who's gon-na talk to me on the phone till the sun comes up? Who's gon-na take your
To Coda
G
Em7
F
place? There ain't no-bod-y bet - ter. Oh, ba-by, ba-by, we be-long to-geth-er. 2. I can't
Verse 2:
Fmaj7
G
Em7
F
3
sleep at night when you are on my mind. Bob-by Wo-mack's on the ra-di-o, sing-ing to me, "If you
Fmaj7
G
N.C.
think you're lone-ly now..." Wait a min-ute, this is too deep, I got-ta change the sta-tion. So I

Fmaj7
G
Em7
F
turn the dial, try'n' to catch a break, and then I hear Ba - by - face, "I on - ly
Fmaj7
G
Em7
Fmaj7
think of you..." and it's break-in' my heart. I'm try'n' to keep it to-geth-er, but I'm fall-ing a - part. I'm feel-ing
G
Em7
Fmaj9
all out of my el - e-ment, throw-ing things, cry-in' try'n' to fi-gure out where the hell I went wrong. The pain re - flect-ed in this
G
Em7
F
D.S. 𝄋 al Coda
song ain't e - ven half of what I'm feel-ing in - side. I need you, need you back in my life. Ba - by,

Coda
Chorus:
Em7
F
Fmaj7
G
we be - long to - geth - er, ba - by. When you left, I lost a part of
Em7
Fmaj9
G
me. It's still so hard to be - lieve. Come back, ba - by, please 'cause
Em7
F
Fmaj7
G
we be - long to - geth - er. Who'm I gon - na lean on when times get rough? Who's gon' talk to
Em7
Fmaj9
G
me till the sun comes up? Who's gon' take your place? There ain't no - bod - y bet - ter. Oh, ba - by, ba - by,

Em7
F
Fmaj7
G
we be - long to - geth - er.
Ooh,
Repeat ad lib. and fade
Em7
Fmaj9
G
Em7
F
ooh,
ooh,
we be - long to-geth - er.

WHAT ABOUT NOW

Words and Music by
BEN MOODY, DAVID HODGES
and JOSH HARTZLER

© 2006 FSMGI (IMRO), SMELLSLIKEMETAL PUBLISHING (BMI), 7 MONTHS OF SHADOWS PUBLISHING (BMI),
BUG MUSIC, INC. (BMI), 12:06 PUBLISHING (BMI) and EMI BLACKWOOD MUSIC, INC. (BMI)
All Rights for FSMGI (IMRO) and SMELLSLIKEMETAL PUBLISHING (BMI) Administered by STATE ONE MUSIC AMERICA (BMI)
All Rights Reserved

Verses 2 & 3:
Am7
Em
2. Change the col - ors of the sky and o - pen up to
3. The sun is break - ing in your eyes to start a new day.
mf
Am7
Em
the ways you made me feel a - live, the ways I loved you.
This bro - ken heart can still sur - vive with a touch of your grace.
Am7
Em
For all the things that nev - er died to make it through the night.
As shad - ows fade in - to the light, I am by your side
D
F
Love will find you.
where love will find you.
What a - bout now?

𝄋 Chorus:
C
C/B
Am7
C/G
What a - bout to - day?
What if you're mak -
F(9)
C/E
Dm7
ing me all that I was meant to be?
What if our love
C
C/B
Am7
C/G
nev - er went a - way?
What if it's lost
F(9)
C/E
Dm7
be - hind words we could nev - er find?
Ba - by, be - fore

To Coda
1.
2.
C/E
F2
Am
Em
F2
it's too late, what a - bout now?
what a - bout now?
Bridge:
Dm
Am
C2
Now that we're here, now that we've come this far, just hold
E7
Dm
Am
on. There is noth - ing to fear, for I am right

F
Dm
be - side you. For all my life,
A5
I am yours. What a - bout now?
Chorus:
Am
C/G
What a - bout to - day? What if you're mak -
mp
F2
C/E
Dm7
ing me all that I was meant to be? What if our love

Am
C/G
F2
nev-er went a-way? What if it's lost be-hind words we could nev-
cresc.
Gsus
D.S. 𝄋 al Coda
Coda
F(9)
er find? What a-bout now?
Ba-by, be-fore
C/E
F(9)
C/E
it's too late, ba-by, be-fore it's too late,
F2
what a-bout now?

WHAT GOES AROUND... COMES AROUND

Words and Music by
TIM MOSLEY, NATE HILLS
and JUSTIN TIMBERLAKE

© 2006 WB MUSIC CORP., VIRGINIA BEACH MUSIC, W.B.M. MUSIC CORP., DANJAHANDZ MUZIK and TENNMAN TUNES
All Rights on behalf of itself and VIRGINIA BEACH MUSIC Administered by WB MUSIC CORP.
All Rights on behalf of itself and DANJAHANDZ MUZIK Administered by W.B.M. CORP.
All Rights for TENNMAN TUNES Administered by UNIVERSAL MUSIC-Z TUNES LLC
All Rights Reserved

C
G
D
had me in the palm of your hand.
may - be I should do the same.
So why your love went a - way,
The fun - ny thing a - bout
Am
C
G
I just can't seem to un - der - stand.
that is, I was read - y to give you my name.
D
Am
C
Thought it was me and you, ba - by, me and you un - til the end,
Thought it was me and you, ba - by, and now, it's all just a shame,
G
D
Am
but I guess I was wrong.
and I guess I was wrong.
Don't wan - na think a - bout it.

C
G
D
Don't wan-na talk a-bout it.
I'm just so sick a-bout it.
Can't be-lieve it's end-ing this way.
Am
C
G
Just so con-fused a-bout it.
Feel-ing the blues a-bout it.
I just can't do with-out ya.
Now,
Pre-chorus:
D
Am
C
tell me, is this fair?
Is this the way it's real-ly
G
D
Am
go-ing down?
Is this how we say good-bye?

C
G
D
Should-'ve known bet - ter when you came a - round that you were gon - na make me cry.
Am
C
G
It's break-ing my heart to watch you run a - round, 'cause I
D
Am
C
know that you're liv - ing a lie. But that's o - kay, ba - by, 'cause in
Chorus:
G
Am
time, you will find... What goes a - round, goes a - round, goes a -

C
G
D
round_ comes all the way___ back a - round.
What goes a -
Am
C
G
round,_ goes a - round,_ goes a - round_ comes all the way___ back a - round.
D
Am
C
What goes a - round,_ goes a - round,_ goes a - round_ comes all the way___
G
D
Am
back a - round.
What goes a - round,_ goes a - round,_ goes a -

C
G
To Coda
1.
N.C.
round_ comes all the way___ back a - round,___ yeah.___
2. Now,
2.
N.C.
Bridge:
___ What goes a - round_ comes a - round,_ yeah.___
___ What goes a - round_ comes a - round._
You should_ know___ that.
What goes a - round_

comes a - round,
yeah.
What goes a - round
D.S. 𝄋 al Coda
comes a - round.
You should know that.
𝄌 Coda
N.C.
1.2.
3.

WHATEVER YOU LIKE

Words and Music by
CLIFFORD HARRIS, DAVID SIEGEL
and JAMES SCHEFFER

© 2008 WARNER-TAMERLANE PUBLISHING CORP., CROWN CLUB PUBLISHING, MERCHANDYZE MUSIC,
EMI BLACKWOOD MUSIC INC. and JIMIPUB MUSIC
All Rights on behalf of itself, CROWN CLUB PUBLISHING and MERCHANDYZE MUSIC Administered by WARNER-TAMERLANE PUBLISHING CORP.
All Rights on behalf of itself and JIMIPUB MUSIC Administered by EMI BLACKWOOD MUSIC INC.
All Rights Reserved

F
C
I said, you can have what - ev - er you like, yeah. Late night
Dm
B♭
sex, so wet, you're so tight. I'll gas up the jet for you to-night and, ba-by, you can go wher-ev-er you like.
sim.
F
C
I said you can go wher-ev-er you like, yeah.
3. I'm talk-in' big boy
Verses 1 & 3:
Dm
B♭
1. An-y-time you want to pick up the tel-e-phone, you know it ain't noth-ing to drop a cou-ple stacks on you.
rides and big boy ice. Let me put this big boy in your life. The thing gets so

F
C
Want it? You could get it, my dear. Five mil - lion dol - lar home, drop Bent-ley's, I swear. Yeah, I
wet and hits so right, let me put this big boy in your life, that's right. I
Dm
B♭
want your bod - y, need your bod - y. Long as you got me, you won't need no - bod - y. You
F
C
want it, I got it, go get it, I'll buy it. Tell them oth - er broke n**-**** be qui - et. Stacks on
Chorus:
Dm
B♭
deck, Pa - trón on ice, and we could pop bot - tles all night and, ba - by, you can have what - ev - er you like.

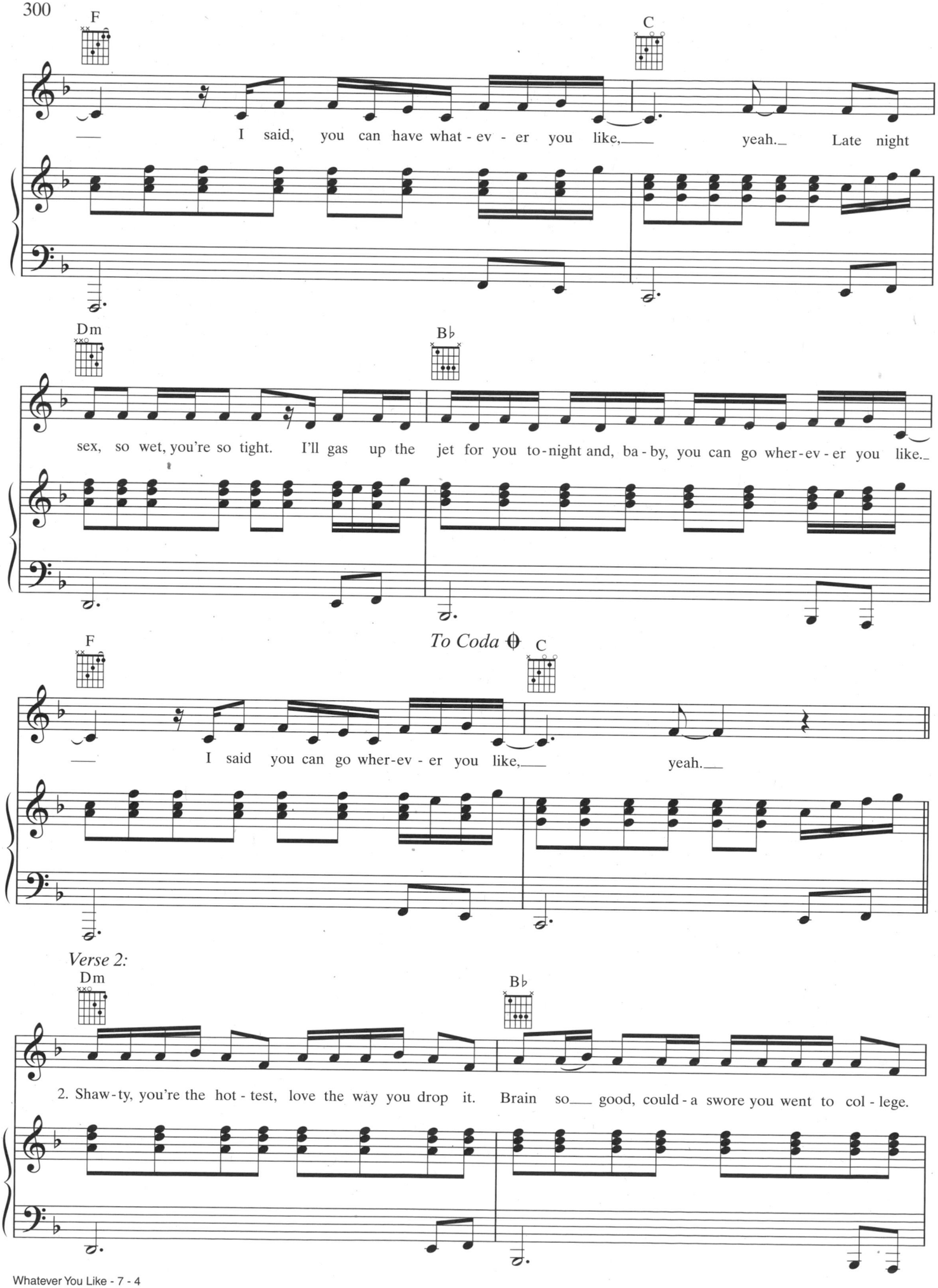
F
C
I said, you can have what - ev - er you like, yeah. Late night
Dm
B♭
sex, so wet, you're so tight. I'll gas up the jet for you to-night and, ba - by, you can go wher-ev - er you like.
To Coda
F
C
I said you can go wher-ev - er you like, yeah.
Verse 2:
Dm
B♭
2. Shaw-ty, you're the hot - test, love the way you drop it. Brain so good, could - a swore you went to col - lege.

F
C
Hun-dred K de-pos-it for va-ca-tions in the trop-ics. Ev-'ry-bod-y know it ain't trick-in' if you got it. You
Dm
B♭
need nev-er ev-er got-ta go in your wal - let, long as I got rub-ber-band banks in my pock - et.
F
C
Five, six rides with rims and a bod-y kit, you ain't got-ta down-grade, you can get what I get.
Dm
B♭
My chick can have what she want and go in an-y store for an-y bag she want. I know she ain't

F
C
nev - er had a man like that, to buy you an - y - thing your heart de - sires like that. Yeah, I

Dm
B♭
want your bod - y, need your bod - y. Long as you got me, you won't need no - bod - y. You

F
C
D.S. 𝄋 al Coda
want it, I got it, go get it, I'll buy it. Tell them oth - er broke n**-**** be qui - et. Stacks on

Coda
C
Dm
yeah.
N.C.
Repeat ad lib. and fade

WILD HORSES

Words and Music by
MICK JAGGER and KEITH RICHARDS

© 1970 (Renewed) ABKCO MUSIC INC., 85 Fifth Avenue, New York, NY 10003
All Rights Reserved

A♭(9)
Cm(9)
A♭(9)
la - dy,
you know who I am.
B♭m(9)
D♭(9)
A♭
You know I can't let you
just slide through my hands.
Chorus:
E♭sus
E♭
B♭m(9)
D♭(9)
And wild
hors - es
mf
A♭
E♭sus
E♭
B♭m(9)
could-n't drag me a - way.
And wild

D♭(9)
A♭(9)
E♭sus
E♭
hors - es
could-n't drag me a - way.
Verse 2:
Cm(9)
A♭(9)
Cm(9)
2. I watched you suf-fer
a dull ach - ing pain.
mp
A♭(9)
B♭m(9)
6
D♭
4
Now you de - cid - ed
A♭(9)
E♭sus
E♭
Cm(9)
to show me the same.
No sweep-ing

A♭(9)
Cm(9)
A♭(9)
ex - its
or off - stage lines
B♭m(9)
D♭(9)
A♭(9)
could make me feel bit - ter
or treat you un - kind.
Chorus:
E♭sus
E♭
B♭m(9)
D♭(9)
And wild
hors - es
mf
A♭(9)
E♭sus
E♭
B♭m(9)
could-n't drag me a - way.
And wild

D♭(9)
A♭(9)
E♭sus
E♭
hors - es
could-n't drag me a - way.
Verse 3:
Cm(9)
A♭(9)
Cm(9)
3. I know I've dreamed you
a sin and a lie.
p
A♭(9)
B♭m(9)
6
D♭(9)
And I have my free - dom,
A♭(9)
E♭sus
E♭
Cm(9)
but I don't have much time.
Faith has been
mp

A♭(9)
Cm(9)
A♭(9)
sev-ered,
and tears must be cried.
B♭m(9)
6
D♭(9)
A♭(9)
So, let's do some liv - ing
af - ter we die.
Chorus:
E♭sus
E♭
B♭m(9)
6
D♭(9)
And wild
hors - es
mf
A♭(9)
E♭sus
E♭
could-n't drag me a - way.

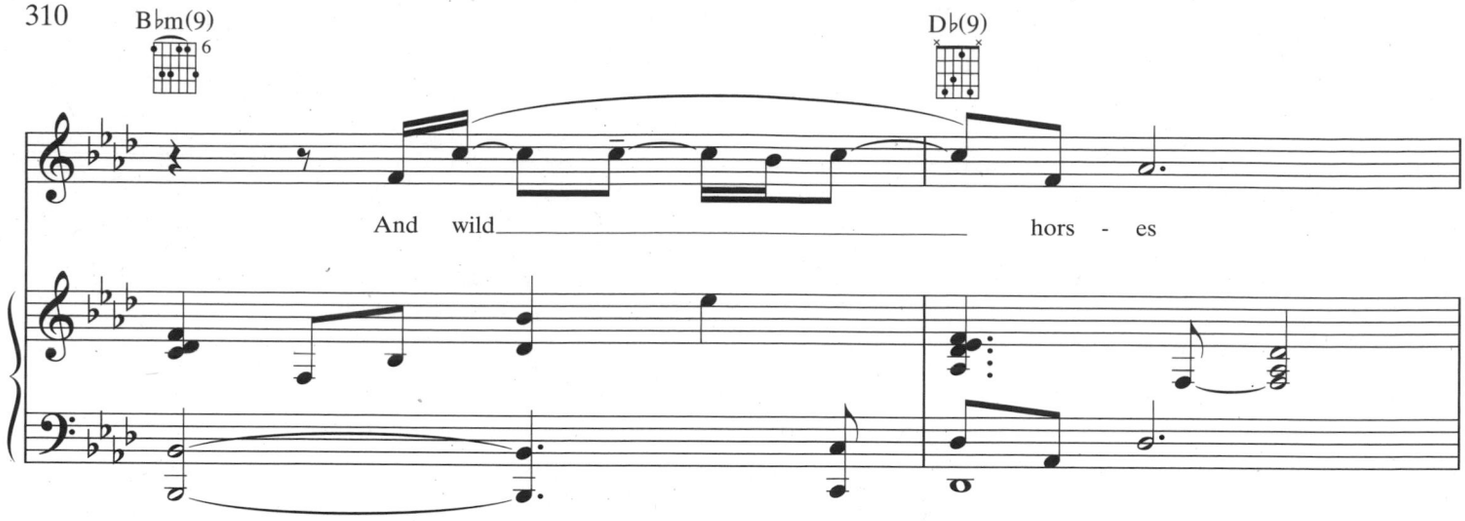
B♭m(9)
D♭(9)
And wild
hors - es

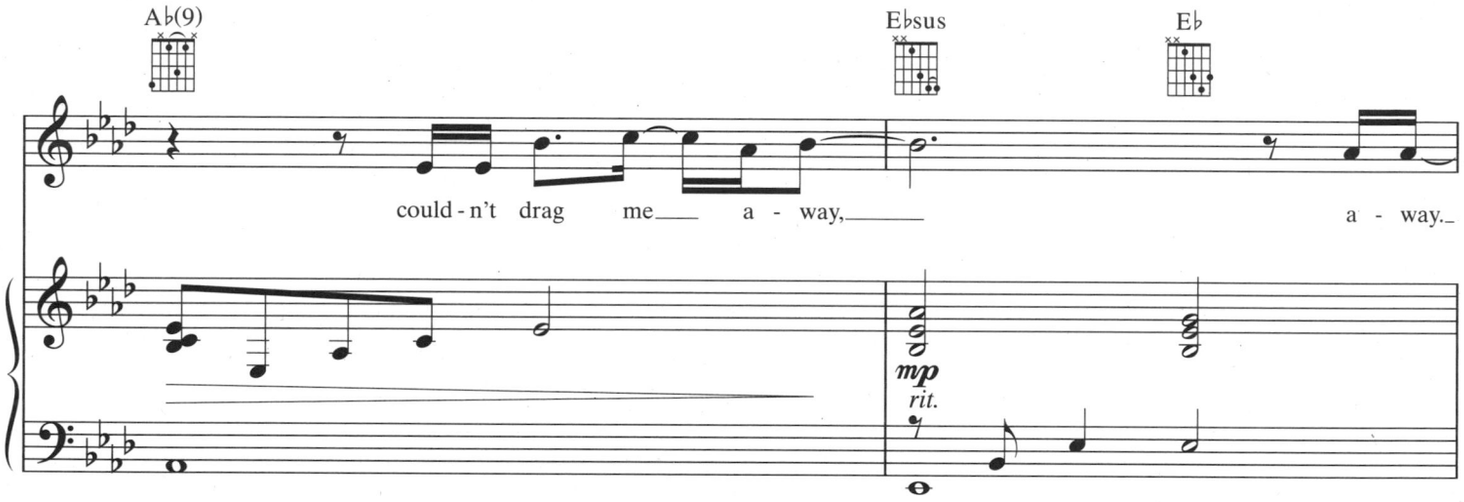
A♭(9)
E♭sus
E♭
could - n't drag me
a - way,
a - way.
mp
rit.

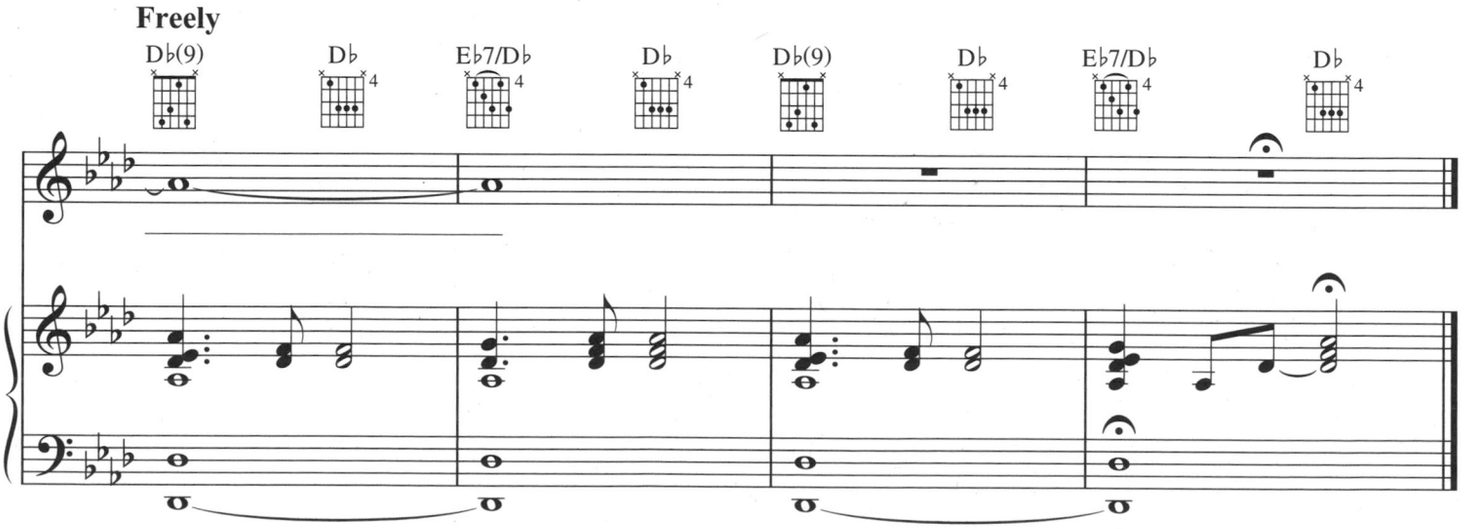
Freely
D♭(9)
D♭
E♭7/D♭
D♭
D♭(9)
D♭
E♭7/D♭
D♭

YOU RAISE ME UP

Words and Music by
ROLF LOVLAND and
BRENDAN GRAHAM

© 2002 UNIVERSAL MUSIC PUBLISHING, A Division of UNIVERSAL MUSIC AS and PEERMUSIC (Ireland) LTD.
All Rights for ROLF LOVLAND and UNIVERSAL MUSIC PUBLISHING Administered in the U.S. and Canada by
UNIVERSAL-POLYGRAM INTERNATIONAL PUBLISHING, INC. (Publishing) and ALFRED MUSIC PUBLISHING CO., INC. (Print)
All Rights Reserved

E♭/B♭
B♭7
E♭
come and sit a while with me. You raise me
cresc.
Chorus:
Cm
B♭/A♭
A♭
E♭/G
B♭/D
up so I can stand on moun - tains. You raise me
mf
Cm
B♭/A♭ A♭
E♭/G
B♭
E♭
A♭(9)/C
up to walk on storm - y seas. I am strong when I am on your
dim.
mp
E♭/B♭ E♭/G A♭(9)
E♭/B♭
B♭7sus
B♭7
E♭
(Violin solo)
shoul - ders. You raise me up to more than I can be.
mf
8vb

F
B♭/F
F
F/A
B♭
Csus
C
B♭(9)/D
B♭
F (9)/A
B♭(9)
F/C
C7sus
F
You raise me
cresc.
Chorus:
Dm
C/B♭ B♭
F/A
C (9)/E
Dm
C/B♭ B♭
up so I can stand on moun - tains. You raise me up to walk on storm - y
f
F/C
Csus
C
F
B♭(9)/D
F/C
F/A
B♭(9)
seas. I am strong when I am on your shoul - ders. You raise me
mf

314
F/C
C7sus
C7
F
B♭/F
F
up to more than I___ can be.
You raise me
f
Chorus:
E♭m
D♭/C♭ C♭
G♭/B♭
D♭(9)/F
E♭m
D♭/C♭ C♭
up so I can stand on moun - tains.
You raise_ me up to walk on storm - y___
G♭/D♭
D♭sus
D♭
G♭
C♭
G♭
E♭m7
seas. I am_ strong when I___ am on_ your shoul - ders.___
You raise me
G♭/D♭
D♭7sus
D♭7
G♭
B♭/D
up to more than I___ can be.
You raise me

E♭m
D♭/C♭ C♭
G♭/B♭
D♭(9)/F
E♭m
D♭/C♭ C♭
up so I can stand on moun - tains. You raise me up to walk on storm - y
G♭/D♭
D♭sus
D♭
G♭
C♭/G♭
G♭
E♭m7
seas. I am strong when I am on your shoul - ders. You raise me
mf
G♭/D♭
D♭7sus
D♭7
E♭m
C♭
up to more than I can be. You raise me
G♭/D♭
D♭7
C♭(9)/G♭
G♭
up to more than I can be.
mp
rit. e dim.
p

YOU PULLED ME THROUGH

Words and Music by
DIANE WARREN

© 2008 REASONGS (ASCAP)
All Rights Reserved

E
G(9)
pulled me back from the edge. Thought I'd reached the end.
strength is what made me strong. You held me and I held on.
Chorus:
D
G2
Bm7
A
When I was drown-ing, when I was so con-fused,
mf
E7sus
G2
D
G2
you, you, you pulled me through. I was in the shad-ows,
Bm7
A
E7sus
1.
G2
lost, noth-ing left to lose. You, you, you pulled me

2.
G2
Bm
F♯7/A♯
you, you pulled me through, out of the dark, in - to your
Bm/A
E(9)/G♯
G(9)
arms, in - to the light. Your love saved my life.
Chorus:
D5
G2
Bm7
When I was drown - ing, when
mp
A
E7sus
G(9)
I was so con - fused, you, oh, you, (you pulled me
When

D
G2
Bm7
through. When I was drown - ing, I was drown - ing, when I was so con - fused,
mf
A
E7sus
G2
I was so con - fused.)
oh, you, oh, you, yeah, you, you pulled me
Bm
A
E(9)/G♯
through. Say, you pulled me,
G
A
D
oh, you pulled me through.
rit.

BRINGING YOU OVER 48,000 TITLES OF TODAY'S HITS AND YESTERDAY'S CLASSICS!

Working on a Dream
Bruce Springsteen
(00-32204)
Book, $19.95

Greatest Hits
Bruce Springsteen
(00-PF9541)
Book, $19.95

Mothership
Led Zeppelin
(00-30381)
Book, $24.95

Dream Theater Keyboard Experience
Dream Theater featuring Jordan Rudess
(00-32032)
Book, $26.95

The Van Halen Keyboard Songbook
Van Halen
(00-27506)
Book, $14.95

In Rainbows
Radiohead
(00-29220)
Book, $19.95

One of the Boys
Katy Perry
(00-31810)
Book, $16.95

Wincing the Night Away
The Shins
(00-28009)
Book, $19.95

American Idiot
Green Day
(00-PFM0506)
Book, $19.95

The Open Door
Evanescence
(00-27640)
Book, $19.95

Vampire Weekend
Vampire Weekend
(00-30733)
Book, $19.95

The Lost Christmas Eve
Trans-Siberian Orchestra
(00-30552) Book, $21.95

SELECTIONS FROM TODAY'S BOX OFFICE HITS

Harry Potter Musical Magic: The First Five Years
Music from Motion Pictures 1-5
(00-32033)
Book, $19.95

The Lord of the Rings: The Fellowship of the Ring
Music by Howard Shore
(00-0659B)
Book, $14.95

Corpse Bride: Selections from the Motion Picture
Music by Danny Elfman
(00-27925)
Book, $16.95

Star Wars: A Musical Journey (Music from Episodes I – VI)
Music by John Williams
(00-28303)
Book, $19.95

The Dark Knight: Selections from the Motion Picture
(00-31866)
Book, $14.95

Indiana Jones and the Kingdom of the Crystal Skull: Selections from the Motion Picture
Music by John Williams
(00-31379)
Book, $12.95

AVAILABLE at YOUR FAVORITE MUSIC RETAILER

Alfred Music Publishing
LEARN • TEACH • PLAY